ENTERPRISE COLLABORATION

INTEGRATED SERIES IN INFORMATION SYSTEMS

Series Editors

Professor Ramesh Sharda
Oklahoma State University

Prof. Dr. Stefan Voß
Universität Hamburg

Other published titles in the series:

ENTERPRISE COLLABORATION
On-Demand Information Exchange for Extended Enterprises

David M. Levermore and Cheng Hsu
Rensselaer Polytechnic Institute, Troy, New York

 Springer

David M. Levermore
Rensselaer Polytechnic Institute
New York, USA

Cheng Hsu
Rensselaer Polytechnic Institute
New York, USA

Library of Congress Control Number: 2006926230

ISBN-10: 0-387-34566-3 (HB)   ISBN-10: 0-387-34567-1 (e-book)
ISBN-13: 978-0387-34566-6 (HB) ISBN-13: 978-0387-34567-3 (e-book)

Printed on acid-free paper.

Printed in the United States of America.

9 8 7 6 5 4 3 2 1

springer.com

Dedication

This book is dedicated to our families

Contents

Preface

Global supply chain is a fact of life in today's world. From the perspective of the First World, this practice reigns in outsourcing of jobs that, in the view of many, threatens a way of life. This argument actually implies that outsourcing represents a fair chance for the Third World to catch up and reverse-leverage through market economy. However, many in the Third World are also opposed to the global market economy from an opposite argument. The fact that matters is, of course, that globalization continues to progress relentlessly in its own momentum, and that the national playing grounds continue to level globally for both Worlds. Would globalization results in the rich nations getting richer and the poor poorer; or would it help the world united in the same economical reason?

The questions that we the researchers could try to answer are a different kind, the kind that leads to the understanding of the elements of "the fittest" in the global competition. For instance, what defines an enterprise's staying power on the top of the food chain, or an economy's ability to design and control the global supply chains, in the long term? Evidently, to understand this ability the field needs to study the engineering prowess required, as much as the finance and management if the history of industrial revolution is any guide. Yet, the study on the engineering of global supply chains has been largely lacking. Traditional enterprise system engineering methods and information technology do not automatically scale up to the massively extended enterprises that global supply chains entail. As a prime example, from the perspective of this book, the problem is illustrated in the limited practice of real-time information exchange across the supply chain – i.e., the field lacks some key elements to enable an enterprise drilling through all tiers of suppliers to coordinate the global schedules. Without this ability, supply chain management would have to rely on managerial control, which is inherently off-line and limited by the manual span of control.

We set out to develop real-time information exchange for massively extended enterprises in the book. Our work started with a simple question: Why the traditional results for global query of autonomous databases do not work sufficiently for supply chains? To answer the question, we draw heavily from our past work on information integration in manufacturing enterprises; that is, we examine the requirements of supply chains in the context of the evolution of enterprise integration, with an ever expanding scale and scope. In this context, we examined the limits of the previous Global Database Query results and the promises of the new extended enterprise approaches, especially the software agent-based methods and the market-style resource allocation models. We realized that the key issues include the independence of the participating databases in the participating enterprises of the supply chains; and that this issue logically extends the previous paradigm of enterprise integration into a new one of enterprises collaboration. The previous paradigm is proven in manufacturing, while the new one is promising for supply chain integration (and indeed, for that matter, in any other similar domains of enterprises collaboration).

It follows, then, that we can formulate a new model which retains the traditional Global Query results, along with their proven promises, to address the new domain for what they can and do best, and devise new attending methods to handle the rest in a synergistic manner. This approach leads to a Two-Stage Collaboration Model, where the first stage, which is new, matches the independent databases for their information provisions and requests in a market-style design, while the second, which is based on proven results, processes the matched, resultant global queries.

The new solution allows enterprises to safely contribute their production databases to collaboration, such as in a supply chain information exchange regime, without having to succumb to an intrusive control model, which has traditionally inhibited the enterprise databases from participating in the collaboration. The solution also supports enterprises to contribute multiple images or personalities of their databases to multiple concurrent collaborating endeavors, as well as to only one. This property attends to the many-to-many relationship between suppliers and supply chains – i.e., the fact that suppliers often sell to more than one buyer or prime. These results distinguish the new model in the field.

In a more general sense, beyond supply chain per se, the new model provides a high-level concept where information owners and seekers collaborate in an economic market to exchange information and facilitate each others' enterprises. The economic paradigm allows participants to choose with whom to trade, and to also define the terms of the transaction.

Accordingly, databases denoted as data providers will not only publish the resources to be shared, but in contrast to traditional global query solutions, also proactively select data subscribers that are looking for information that the databases contain. The economic market works towards self-allocation or self-regulation of resources for optimal global utilization. In the general context, the present work holds promises for application domains that employ database query-level information fusion and on-demand exchange of information resources.

In summary, the book analyzes the evolution of Enterprise Integration from the perspective of the Two-Stage Collaboration Model, and reviews the related results in the literature. Supply chain integration provides a context for these discussions. A general agent-based conceptual model is then developed to usher in the main result of the book. On this basis, the rest of the book is devoted to the complete development of the Two-Stage Collaboration Model. The first stage is analytically justified on its computing performance and unique properties, vis-à-vis the previous results in the fields of matchmaking and global database query. A prototype and laboratory testing are also included to illustrate the technical feasibility and soundness of the new model.

The book is based on David's unpublished dissertation at Rensselaer Polytechnic Institute, Troy, NY 12180-3590, with substantive revision and extension.

April 20, 2006

Acknowledgments

The authors wish to thank Professor Gilbert Babin of the HEC, Montréal, whose technical insight made the results on information matching possible. We also wish to thank the other members of David's doctoral committee, who served along with Cheng: Professors William Wallace, Mark Embrechts, and Christopher Carothers, for their assistance to David's dissertation. Finally, we wish to thank the publisher, Mr. Gary Folven, and the reviewers of the book and the series editors for their recommendation and approval to publish this book.

Chapter 1

ENTERPRISE COLLABORATION
A Solution for Supply Chain Integration and Beyond

1. THE EVOLUTION OF ENTERPRISE INTEGRATION

Enterprise Integration is arguably originated in post-Industrial Revolution manufacturing. Whereas Industrial Revolution developed standardization – standard parts, standard bill-of-materials, and even standard machines and fabrication processes, therefore the breakthroughs beyond it have come mainly from building ever-larger scale of flexibility to remove the drawbacks of standardization from ever-larger scale of manufacturing systems. Integration is the means to scale up and build flexibility; and information and information technology are the key enablers to achieving integration. The field has witnessed the development of the concrete results for integrating standardized components, sub-systems, and systems of manufacturing enterprises. It has also witnessed the ensuing development of the scaling up of the manufacturing enterprises into the extended enterprises along supply chains, which lack strong standardization. Now, it is even witnessing the application of Enterprise Integration to service in general, including the emerging visions of On-Demand Business/Service. Along with this development, the field is also experiencing a renaissance of service enterprise engineering through information.

In retrospect, much of what happened in the field of manufacturing since 1970's can be described as the milestones of Enterprise Integration. The effort started with the computerization of engineering design (e.g., CAD/CAE/CAPP – or, computer-aided design/engineering/process planning) and manufacturing facilities (e.g., CAM/MES/FMS – or, computer-aided manufacturing/manufacturing executive systems/flexible manufacturing system), evolved into the integration of islands of automation for the enterprise (e.g., CE/Concurrent Engineering, CIM/Computer-Integrated Manufacturing, and ERP/Enterprise Resources Planning), and continued today to cover the extended enterprises of the whole product life cycle (e.g., PLCM/Product Life Cycle Management and e-Engineering). The vision of product life cycle naturally brings the demand chains and supply chains into the concern of the integration, and hence espouses the push for on-demand products and on-demand production across all organizations involved in the extended enterprises.

Integration within an organization is reasonably mature, technologically speaking. The field has accumulated impressive results in software, hardware, and telecommunications to connect enterprise processes and resources. On this basis, enterprises can turn their sequential processes into concurrent to reduce transaction cost and cycle time. They can also strive to satisfy their customers with personalized (mass-customization) services and products to expand the market. A proof of the maturity is that, the results of enterprise integration (including enterprise system engineering) are diffusing from manufacturing into service sectors. A prime case in point is the notion of On-Demand Business and On-Demand Service, which draw from the previous on-demand manufacturing results such as agile manufacturing.

Integration across organizations, on the other hand, faces formidable organizational issues. In the past, supply chain integration, for instance, relied on contractual agreements to exchange information and coordinate schedules between the producers of parts/products and the users of them. Other efforts to reconcile enterprise processes across organizations have similarly limited to the level of human managerial control as opposed to technically based systems integration. Companies such as Wal-Mart and Cisco have invested heavily to effect technical integration to their supply chains. Due to these efforts, the field has witnessed the maturing of technology for the direct integration of immediate partners – e.g., the prime and its first tier suppliers. To "drill through" multiple tiers of suppliers remains a challenge to the field. The problems stem not only from the scalability of the previous results for recursive connection of partners along the open-ended supply chain, but also from the fact that the relationship between the primes and the suppliers are many-to-many – or, a partner belongs to more than one demand chain and supply chain at any one point and at any one time. The issues of openness, scalability, and flexibility challenge fundamentally the technology of enterprise integration.

Take Wal-Mart and Warner-Lambert as an example. The extended enterprise process of Warner-Lambert's supplying of the product Listerine to Wal-Mart could be facilitated by EDI (electronic data interchange), the Internet-based solutions, or some industrial exchanges, as three representative technologies of enterprise integration. The first requires direct "hand-shaking" arrangements (e.g., API – application programs interchange) between the Wal-Mart systems (e.g., inventory replenishment) and the Warner-Lambert's (e.g., order processing) using proprietary software and value-added dedicated network. The connection cannot be readily expanded to include other systems in the process or other processes of the extended enterprise, without multiplying the effort. Furthermore, for each additional trading partner to join the system, (n-1) additional connections need to be developed with similar effort; where n is the total number of partners. Therefore, the total number of connections to be established with the EDI approach for a supply chain of n partners, in general, is $n(n-1)/2$.

An Internet-based solution, such as the well-known CFAR project in late 1990's – see Fig. 1-1, can remove the limitations due to value-added networks, but cannot remove much of other limitations. For instance, the CFAR project linked Wal-Mart's forecasting information to Warner-Lambert's SAP/R3 system through dedicated protocols and routines; and yet this linkage did not address its extension to other systems at Warner-Lambert or elsewhere that might benefit from the same information. That is, the new connection as shown in the dashed line in the figure is the result of the process-to-process (involving inter-operation of enterprise databases) collaboration; which can replace the previous EDI level connections (the solid lines) but cannot allow other processes to join readily. The savings over the EDI arose mainly from the openness and scalability of the Internet: in this case, only one additional connection is required of each new partner - from the partner to the Internet. The total number of connections is precisely n, the number of partners included in the supply chain. The connection itself, however, still involves high transaction cost and face organizational barriers (i.e., the issues and difficulties associated with opening up each organization's enterprise systems for others to inter-operate – such as control, security, and maintenance).

Example: Collaboration (the CFAR case)

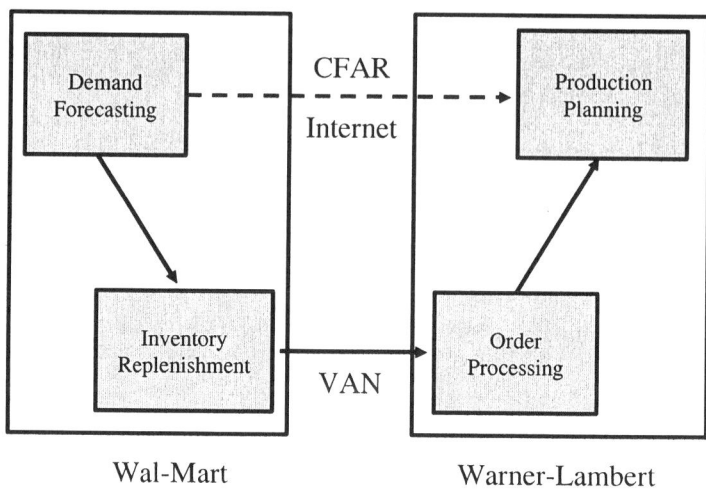

Figure 1-1. Enterprise Collaboration at the Process Level, the CFAR case

Finally, the latest industrial exchange approach, such as the automotive Covisint.com, promises to support concurrent connection of suppliers from multiple tiers for the primes that own the exchange. In this approach, all participants of the supply chains meet at the virtual marketplace and transact (buy-sell negotiation and agreement) by using the same set of global protocols and tools. However, the transaction does not include the connection of the participants' enterprise systems – i.e., the degree of information sharing achieved in this approach is still below the high watermark that CFAR reached. In particular, enterprise databases are not inter-operable under the current technology of industrial exchanges. New results are required to bring the functionality of the industrial exchange approach to a level of global database query while retain the approach's relatively low transaction cost and cycle time, and relatively high openness and scalability.

Notwithstanding the difficulties in organizational and technical arenas, enterprise collaboration is clearly on the rise and will continue to push the envelope as far as the continuing progress of enterprise integration technology can support. We show below two thought models, one for the enterprise integration within an organization and the other the collaboration across organizations. Both thought models represent our view of the design metaphysics that has been driving the progress of the field.

The Model of Enterprise Integration

- Objective: reduce transaction cost and cycle time
- Means: Use open and scalable information technology and systems to:
  - Connect tasks with resources and information
  - Simplify and streamline processes and/or workflows (re-engineering)
- Share/inter-operate human and non-human resources (data, knowledge and processes)
  - Convert sequential processes into concurrent
- Scope: the whole enterprise or clearly defined and administered extended enterprise (e.g., along demand chains and supply chains)

The Model of Enterprise Collaboration

- Objective: reduce societal transaction cost and cycle time
- Means: seek collaboration from three perspectives,
  - Follow the value chain. (Apply the enterprise integration model to extended enterprises along aggregate demand/supply chains.)
  - Put the Person at the Center. (Alter the societal value chain to connect businesses along the life cycle requirements of a person.)
  - Serve the Whole Enterprise (extended). (Align business services with the client's life cycle requirements of an enterprise.)
- Scope: open and scalable extended enterprises (e.g., along societal value chains)

The evolution is reflected in the scope of integration. Organizationally, the scope is expanding away from the origin that requires a clear administrative authority for the entire enterprise; which includes the case of single firms and that of multiple partners bonded with definitive business contracts for the effort. The bonding gives way in the evolution to increasingly relaxed community agreements that govern more the classes of individual, random transactions than the wholesale coverage of products and processes. Conversely, with this relaxation on authority, partners are able to push for increasingly more grand integration across organizations. As the organizational scope expanding, so must the technology of integration. The evolution inevitably makes openness and scalability the key concept in the development of new technologies. The Internet showcases the power of this concept beyond any doubt. The continuing movement toward embracing open source code, not just the recent adoption of Linux by much of the industry, as evidenced in IBM and other industry leaders, further illustrates this point.

Our work as reported in this book contributes to a core element of the new technology called for by the continuing evolution; that is, the on-demand information exchange among a large number of databases owned by a large number of collaborating enterprises. In other words, the work deals with *the global query aspect of the inter-operation of massively distributed, autonomous, and heterogeneous databases*; which is the technical literature to which the work belongs. From this point on, we focus on the technical nature of the on-demand information exchange problem in the context of Enterprise Integration and Enterprise Collaboration, as defined above. We discuss the goal of the work from this particular perspective in the next section, before we discuss the research problem and describe what we have accomplished.

2. ON-DEMAND INFORMATION EXCHANGE: THE GOAL

Simply put, the goal is to allow collaborating participants to query each other's enterprise databases without hindering their control and operation of their own systems, nor paying prohibiting transaction cost and cycle time. The control and cost issues also determine the openness and scalability of enterprise collaboration; i.e., how the collaborating community accommodates new partners, and how the partners can join or leave multiple such communities. Looking conversely, the above "without-nor" clause actually describes the limits of the previous results and indicates the practical contributions of the new work. With this ability, enterprises can move a step forward in their collaboration, such as drilling through the supply chain to coordinate their schedules and connect their processes.

To be sure, supply chains are always concerned with information exchange among trading partners. Previous results already promised the integrated view of critical functions including, among others, purchasing, demand management, quality management and manufacturing planning (Wisner and Tan 2000). The problem is, they do not afford participants real-time and online data throughout the supply chain. At most, they rely on particular hand-shaking arrangements such as those illustrated in the CFAR project to provide fixed, pre-determined information exchange; or they contend with summary data or "catalog" data only – such as the MESChain system (Cingil and Dogac 2001). Therefore, the integrated view of critical functions attainable is confined to certain finite templates. Integrated views that are attainable for custom needs at random moments really require on-demand information exchange.

Certainly, on-demand information exchange is also available in traditional information technology used for enterprise integration. The primary case of such results is global database query; which allows users to share information on-demand, in real-time across several databases. The problem is the scope: traditional global data query typically requires a single authority over all databases involved and incurs significant effort to design (e.g., schema integration), implement, and maintain the system – i.e., suitable basically for integration within a single organization. When applied to enterprise collaboration, many organizations could not or would not open up their production databases to abide by such a regime for trading partners, let alone commit to open-ended implementation. For this reason global database query has not been widely employed in supply chains or industrial exchanges; although the technology is best suited for acquiring of integrated views. As proven in traditional enterprise integration, global database query promises "deeper" information sharing at the enterprise database level than the customary trading of flat documents, e.g., purchase orders and invoices, found in the industry, that supply chains rely. Clearly, the field needs to make global database query a more open and scalable technology to suit the need of enterprise collaboration.

Yet, to become more open and scalable the traditional paradigm of global database query must evolve; it must shed its traditional one-sided command structure, where information retrievals are the only type of database queries that dominate the user needs and the design of the control structure. In this paradigm, the participating databases are passive subjects of search in which they are completely open to all users' search (barring some hard-coded security checks) at all time. Virtually, the only control they have over their contents against the search is to withdraw from the global query system altogether. In such a retrieval-dominated one-sided paradigm, the design is necessarily oriented toward optimizing the information retrieval process at the expenses of the autonomy of the participating databases. Therefore, even when the traditional technology considers local autonomy, the consideration still requires participating databases to surrender their control to a global regime, as to when and what information is searchable to whom.

Enterprise collaboration requires a new paradigm where the participating databases control their provision of information on demand, just like users control their information requests on demand. Instead of just being passive objects of global search, databases are regarded as proactive information providers that also seek users to subscribe to their information. This is a two-sided command structure with the databases (information providers) being an equal participant to users (information requesters). In this paradigm, certain traditional elements are still valid. In particular, it must simplify the information integration process and reduce the effort required to resolve semantic differences across databases, in the face of the heterogeneity and autonomy that are inherent to on-demand information exchanges (e.g., a global view of the community). It must afford participants an acceptable process by which they join the system (e.g., registration) and a reasonable mechanism by which they use the system (e.g., global query language and local interface). In addition, it must afford the participants the ability to cooperate and share databases on-demand and in real-time, as well as the capability to control what information is shared, how it is shared, when and to whom; rather than *carte blanche* to any trading partner that has access to the information exchange community.

Finally, on the basis of these new capabilities, the new paradigm should support an enterprise database joining multiple information exchange communities with distinct "personalities" at the same time. For example, a manufacturer's inventory database may be of concern to a number of trading partners in different supply chains of different primes (owned separately by, e.g., Wal-Mart and Bloomingdale). Each chain may require different semantics of the same inventory database when exchange information. Each model of data semantics would give rise to a personality of the database.

The new paradigm of global database query can be comprehended from other perspectives of enterprise collaboration, as well. Homeland security is such an example. As mandated by law, multiple federal agencies must sense, exchange and fuse information from across the security community. Moreover, the job of gathering information also extends to other agencies at all levels of government and even to companies and persons in the private sector. Certainly, this information exchange, rather collaboration, has to be dynamic, virtual, and voluntary. Information should flow freely, but still be secure and of assured integrity; it must be readily accessible – which means requested and offered on-demand, and not dependent on any centralized authority. Furthermore, the facilitating infrastructure must be platform agnostic and accept diverse information resources. All these characteristics and requirements point to a new global database query problem that we described above.

Therefore, in this book, we develop a new global database query technology to achieve the goal of on-demand information exchange as a tool for enterprise collaboration. The new technology is based on a new paradigm of participatory databases, where the databases are **independent** as opposed to being controllable by a global authority as the traditional regime assumes; and the new technology retains the basic promises of traditional global databases query while accomplishing a new level of openness and scalability. To this end, the particular solution approach developed combines the established results from both the global database query field and the e-business exchange field, and integrates them with original results on information matching and processing that the problem requires. We refer to the complete solution the *Two-Stage Collaboration Model*, which extends traditional global query to meet the requirements of on-demand information exchange. The model introduces the concepts of publication queries (information offers) and subscription queries (information requests) at the user level, and thereby characterizes its two-sidedness. The first stage establishes the required global queries on demand, and the second executes the queries.

3. TWO-STAGE COLLABORATION MODEL: THE RESEARCH AND SOLUTION

We explain in this section why these two stages are needed, and how the e-business exchange results can help remove the limits on the openness and scalability of the traditional global query results. First, we elaborate on these limits to show that they are fundamentally pegged to a one-sided command structure, as mentioned above. It follows, then, that opening it up leads naturally to a market regime at the front-end of query formulation. Finally, we show that a particular model of the traditional global query results is amenable to coupling with the exchange approach and the integration of both can give rise to a solution to the on-demand information exchange problem with the required properties.

The field of Global Query of autonomous databases offers maximum on-demand information exchange among traditional results for enterprise integration within single organizations. It faces a few difficult issues including especially the hard problem of integrating and maintaining massively distributed and heterogeneous data models. To solve the problem and other related issues, the distributed databases are typically configured as components of a strict search regime, subservient to a single authority, which rigorously defines and maintains the global database query infrastructure. Essentially, this regime tends to flounder if the authority is distributed since, in part, the required integration of schemas will become impractical in this situation. This is a common problem facing the previous results in this field, such as schema integration approaches, federated and multi-database systems and peer-to-peer networks.

The tenuous nature of the integration environments extends to the technical approaches to query processing, schema integration, transaction processing, concurrency control and other aspects. The enabling algorithms for query processing, for example, depend on heuristic search methodologies that degrade, become exponentially complex, or even intractable, when the number of databases in the integration environment increases. This may be caused by a number of reasons, such as the required statistics for query processing operations may not be provided by the associated databases, or latency on communication network may hinder these operations. The problem is exacerbated when the environments increases the demand for a greater degree of heterogeneity and autonomy. When the transaction cost imposed on local databases to join a global query system is already high, the prospect of administering them for integration into different such global query systems can be prohibitive. When new databases are added, most of the previous results would have to require significant modifications or redesign to the integration environments, such as creating new pair-wise external schemas to connect the new databases with the old. The complexity tends to be n(n-1). An exception is the Metadatabase results that we use for the Two-Stage Collaboration Model; as will be discussed later.

We examine more closely three representative technologies from the traditional field: Schema Integration, Multi-Database Languages and Federated Database Systems. The degree of autonomy, heterogeneity and distribution varies for these particular integration methods, and so influences their global query capabilities.

Schema integration (Batini, Lenzerini et al. 1986) consolidates the data models of multiple distributed systems into a common, unified schema. This approach offers system transparency, and resolves semantic conflicts that may exist among the distributed systems. It however limits the autonomy of local systems through its imposing the global schema or the global administrator on the local databases. An additional concern relates to the administration of the common schema, which requires a typically manual process to integrate schemas, given the human input required to resolve the semantic, structural and behavioral conflicts. This process clearly increases in difficulty in at least a polynomial manner as the number of local schemas to be integrated grows.

Federated database management systems (Sheth and Larson 1990) provide greater flexibility for distributed databases due to the extended, five-level schema architecture. However, the degree of autonomy of the local system is dependent on the type of federation, that is, whether it is a loosely or tightly coupled federation. Tightly coupled federations mimic the schema integration approach mentioned above, since the global administrator dictates the contents of the federated schema. The departure from the schema integration approach is in the amount of data provided to the global controller – this needs not be the complete data model, but can be fragments that are denoted as export schemas for global query. It should be pointed out that the designation of the export schemas is fixed, not on-demand. On the other hand, in loosely coupled federations, multiple schemas are created and managed by local administrators, which may subsequently lead to redundancies in the federation. The schemas so created are typically less complex than those in tightly-coupled federations, and additionally tend to be brittle and more easily compromised. Moreover, these schemas though integrated are primarily read-only and typically cannot process inserts, deletes, or updates on the schema, since there is no complete ownership of the federated schemas. In any case, the administration of the schemas requires manual processing to reconcile semantics and cascade changes, and hence involve significant cost. This transaction cost hinders on-demand information exchange as well as the openness and scalability of the integration environment.

Multi-database languages (Litwin 1985) are applied to pre-existing heterogeneous database environments that lack a global controller or global schema. No integration measures are taken to consolidate the databases; rather, the multi-database language incorporates the necessary constructs to query the participating databases. Multi-database languages provide for greater autonomy, heterogeneity and distribution of databases, at the expense of requiring the users to possess greater knowledge of the overall database environment, such that users must know where specific data reside to correctly formulate the global queries and perform joins, scans on database relations, and other operations.

Apart from the above three approaches, the Metadatabase Model (Hsu 1996) represents a different thinking to integrating and managing the global semantics. Instead of creating layered structures of fixed schemas, it focuses on local data models and treats them as enterprise metadata (along with contextual knowledge) that are integrated and administered as an enterprise database. The Metadatabase is the repository of the enterprise metadata. Local data models are added, deleted, and modified as metadata tuples to the relations in the Metadatabase, and thereby afford the Metadatabase the same openness and scalability in accommodating local data models as relational databases do for ordinary records. As such, it is an information resources management system that facilitates the integration of distributed, heterogeneous and autonomous information systems. The Metadatabase architecture is comprised of the Metadatabase, the Metadatabase Management System (MDBMS), the Metadatabase Global Query System (MGQS), the Metadatabase Query Language (MQL), and the Rule-Based Programming Environment (ROPE).

The Global Information Resources Dictionary (GIRD) represents the logical structure of the Metadatabase – its schema. The representation method is based directly on the Two-Stage Entity-Relationship (TSER) model and its attendant modeling methodology. The TSER model is a generic extension to the standard Entity-Relationship-Attribute model that includes object concepts and rule-base concept for data and knowledge modeling. All local data models are represented in TSER (in a way amenable to using a Computer-Aided Software Engineering) during the registration process, and then populated into the Metadatabase. In this way, TSER is the conceptual limit of what kind of systems the Metadatabase Model can accommodate and with how much transaction cost. The MDBMS manages and processes the Metadatabase, including searching on the metadata it contains. MGQS and MQL provide ad-hoc query capabilities for managing the local databases. MGQS avails the enterprise user with a model-assisted approach to query formulation, where the user can select in a "point and click" manner the metadata items that pertain to the information of interest, and MGQS produces a completely formulated and optimized global query. The underlying capabilities of MGQS are provided by the non-procedural query language MQL, a global query language that is an extension of SQL but supports queries across distributed and heterogeneous local systems with different schemata as well as different data semantics. MGQS translate the MQL expressions into multitude of local-bound sub-queries, which are expressed in local data languages (such as SQL). While all other components are co-located with the Metadatabase, ROPE - the architecture of software shells – is distributed at local databases to connect them according to the global model (data and contextual knowledge). ROPE inter-operates between the Metadatabase and local databases, as well as among local systems. It submits sub-queries to the local databases involved in the global query for local processing, and transfers the results back to the MGQS for assembly. We discuss further details of the Metadatabase Model in Chapter 2.

More recent results address some aspects of the on-demand information exchange problem more than the traditional global query field has provided, but they also lack in other aspects. Web Service architectures and P2P networks are emerging as *de facto* standards for data integration and information sharing in today's enterprise networks. Mainstream file sharing networks such as Napster and Gnutella, popularized P2P networks and exposed the technology to a wider community of users. A significant disadvantage of P2P networks in this regard, however was the lack of a fine-grained approach to file sharing; if a resource was shared, all elements within that resource are available to the entire community with no way to restrict access to specific users, and no way to allocate resources for different groups. Furthermore, P2P networks do not readily support global query beyond parametrical keyword searching.

Web Service architectures provide a collection of communication protocols and associated language specifications that offer an open and standards-based method for information integration. Using Web Services, companies with disparate information technologies are able to share data by using these protocols and language specifications; accordingly, when Web Services are exposed to a wide audience, it presents the opportunity to engage potential customers and business partners, who can automatically and seamlessly integrate these services into their own operations. However, global data semantics is largely lacking, or taken as a given; that is, the semantics issues are left for the participants to interpret, as well as to figure out the discrepancies and reconcile them. This approach also requires participants to adopt these standards to the extent of replacing their legacy and proprietary technologies.

However, recent progress has also shed light on how to open up the information retrieval-dominated, one-sided paradigm and convert it to the two-sided paradigm of participatory database query. In particular, the market-based systems (Clearwater 1996) offer some new thinking for this problem; that is, on-demand information exchange is consistent with the basic characteristics of transactions on a market between information providers and information requesters. The database participatory query, therefore, can be interpreted as a matching of information offering queries and information requesting queries at the first stage, followed by the execution of the matched queries at the second stage. Conceptually, the data integration task in enterprise collaboration is formulated as a **distributed resource allocation problem**, and the two stages constitute a solution to the problem.

The market finds a solution, or an optimal distribution of resources, in the balance between the supply (data resources provision) and demand (information retrieval queries). An optimal allocation of resources needs not be found; in which case, queries may need to be refined, or the data may not be available. This approach reduces the complexity of large scale optimization to a function of *self-regulation* according to certain measure of value embedded in the users (which may include availability and performance).

Self-regulation is in the nature of a market-based approach. However, it is also arguably necessary for participatory database query because of the intricate differences that exist across myriad distributed database systems in a collaboration environment. The attempt to devise and deploy a top-down synchronization mechanism to administer this on-demand participation of databases would be a difficult, if not impossible, undertaking. With self-regulation, participating databases determine their own conditional participation in global query, and to conditionally provide access to their information resources. They define their association within the global query infrastructure, to freely and voluntarily join, and disjoin without disruption of a pre-existing and ongoing global query sessions, and without reliance on a centralized controller to regulate this process. They also possess the capability to make public the data resources of their own choosing at any time, and modify the publication at any time, and still retain full membership of the collaborating community. These critical capabilities of collaboration are unavailable in any of the above traditional approaches, including the Metadatabase Model.

From the traditional global query results to the recent market-based systems, a promising solution approach is emerging to implement the Two-Stage Collaboration Model, under the two-sided participatory database query paradigm, for on-demand information exchange. That is, a market design can be coupled with the Metadatabase Model to provide the required two stages. The design will allow participants to collaborate voluntarily in an information exchange, to choose with whom to trade, and to also define the terms of the transaction. Accordingly, data publishers publish the resources to be shared, and in contrast to traditional global query solutions, seek data subscribers that are looking for information that the databases contain. The market matches the publishers and subscribers on their own terms (offering queries and requesting queries) through a new, particular information matching method, and executes the allocated resources using the extended Metadatabase Model. The new information matching method and the extensions to the Metadatabase Model are developed in the research.

4. INTEGRATION OF A MARKET WITH THE METADATABASE: THE RESULTS

The TSCM results for on-demand information exchange are the focus of the book. However, they are also generalized into a model for the allocation of enterprise resources, the Enterprise Resources Market (ERM) model. The development of this general model is reported in (Hsu 2002; Hsu and Carothers 2003; Hsu and Carothers 2004; Hsu, Carothers et al. 2005), which is also summarized in Chapter 3 of the book. The general model provides a conceptual design of an agent-based market, which is applicable to certain on-demand system engineering problem for both Enterprise Integration and Enterprise Collaboration. Insofar as the particular information matching method is consistent with an agent-based design, the TSCM results represent a particular instantiation of the general ERM approach.

For the purpose of the TSCM, the Participatory Database Query problem can be described succinctly as the global query of a loose collection of independent databases whose participation in information exchange and sharing is controlled by the databases. Accordingly, we define Collaboration to mean the following conditions of Global Query, which characterize the difference between this extended work and the previous results:

- *Participant*: a single or a cluster of data resources that controls its own participation in the Community and the information contents with which it participates; responsible for its own data models; and can independently issue information requests and/or information offers. (This definition is stronger than the usual notion of autonomy in the literature of databases.)
- *Community:* a collection of participants which joins through a Community-sanctioned registration process and subscribes to a Community-sanctioned protocol of collaboration.
- *On-Demand:* The initiation of a request and/or an offer (the publication and subscription for information exchange) by a participant can start at any time and last for any duration, and the participation and the information contents of participation can change at any time.
- *Collaborators:* the matched information requests and information offers (or the participants who initiated these matched requests/offers).

We do not impose conditions on the number of information sources, nor prescribe the nature of their networking, data semantics, and the regime of data processing (such as ebXML or XQuery) in this definition. These important issues belong to the design of the specific solution algorithms for particular application domains and requirements, since they define the particularization of the general model. The definition allows for peer-to-peer collaboration as well as a regime that imposes a controlling global administrator. Nonetheless, a minimum (virtual) global site that implements the registration process is required.

The particular TSCM methods are developed from three bases: first, a conceptual framework in ERM; second, the Metadatabase Model discussed above; and third, new results developed in this work (i.e., exMQL, the Blackboard and Query Database, and exMGQS – see below). The general purpose ERM concept employs software agents to perform matching and other market functions. Like most other market models, it also treats matching and global query as two separate models and uses completely separate methods to conduct them. In contrast, for on-demand information exchange, the TSCM replaces software agents with a unified Metadata Query Language, called exMQL; which performs both matching and global query. Towards this end, the previous Metadatabase model serves as the basic representation method for the novel design of the new query database, and thereby integrates the query language, query processing, and matching into a simplified regime.

For matching information collaborators, exMQL formulates both information requests and information offers as database queries and save them into a Query Database (which replaces the Agent-Base of the general ERM, or the Agent Community in the general literature of agents). The basic semantics of exMQL is also the basic structure (schema) of the query database. With this design, processing a query against the query database is to perform a matching for finding the right information collaborators. The metadata semantics includes both data and rules found in information requests and offers, and hence the query database schema and the metadata language both include rules as well as data. The rule component is an extension to the previous matching methods of e-business and previous query languages. After the optimal participants are determined from the matching, the language also executes the requests at the local sites of the matched offers across the community – for global query processing.

Finally, this new method results in a new simplified design for the Blackboard that artificial markets, including the ERM, always need. The design reduces the usually complicated, custom-developed Blackboard to an off-the-shelf database management system (DBMS) that performs all matching and global query functions in standard SQL and PL/SQL. In addition, the design for the open and scalable common schema and the efficient computing onboard the sensors are also contributions of this paper. We might also mention that the new model does not require a price mechanism. The mere existence of a motive to cooperate among participants would suffice.

4.1   The basic logic of the two-stage solution approach

- The *objective function*: the maximization of the total (perceived) value of information resources.
- The *constraints*: the transaction requirements and data semantics of tasks (information requests and offers of the global query processing).
- A *feasible solution*: a match of information offers (database views) with requests (global queries).
- The *optimization*: The execution of a request for information or a provision of information.

- ***Stage 1***: match requests with offers to find the right information collaborators; i.e., determine the optimal alignment of participants (users and/or databases/sensor networks) for a global query processing task.
- ***Stage 2***: execute the global query task; i.e., choose the suitable query processing regime to distribute the task to participants and process it at the local sites, and then assemble the query results for the user.

The basic logic of this two-stage collaboration is depicted in Fig. 1-2, a subscriber submits a request to the Blackboard, and a publisher submits an offer. The Blackboard will then execute a search on the database looking for a match to the request, and a match to the offer. If the request matches an existing offer, then the Blackboard assigns (awards) the processing of the request to the associated export database, which is an image (personality) of the local enterprise database. The query is delivered to the export database for processing, is executed, and the results are returned to the subscriber via the Blackboard.

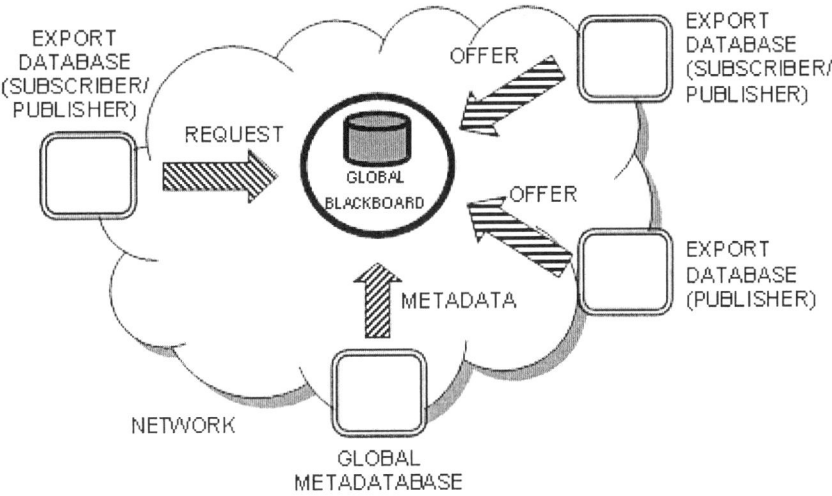

Figure 1-2. Conceptual Overview of the Two Stage Collaboration Model

Therefore, the particular new results developed for the TSCM include the algorithms and architecture necessary to deploy the Blackboard and Export Database, in addition to the communication protocols necessary to mobilize these components. The algorithms that are developed include the Matching, Combination Matching and Constraint Matching Algorithms in Chapter 4, and those required to support the transformation and execution of the queries from exMQL to the native language of the export database in Chapter 6. The query matching algorithm allocates query processing jobs to the export database that best matches the supplied query. The process, however, may involve a round of negotiation for the query processing job if multiple publishers respond to a single request (see Chapter 4).

Thus far, in this chapter, we have provided an overview of the Enterprise Collaboration problem, and in this context formulated the conceptual and technical nature of the on-demand information exchange problem and its Two-Stage Collaboration Model solution. We have also provided an overview of the related literature to shed light on the research nature of the work. The remainder of this book is divided into three main areas: (1) the general background of the research problem, Chapter 2, and the general market model of ERM, Chapter 3; (2) the execution methods of the TSCM in Chapters 4, 5, and 6; and (3) the analysis of the solution and comparison to previous results in Chapters 7 and 8.

In particular, Chapter 2 provides a detailed literature review of the field, placing emphasis on the nascent research in Market-Based Resource Allocation and Global Query, as well as the Metadatabase research since it forms the core of the TSCM. The TSCM design is compared to previous Global Query results on this basis. In Chapter 3 the concepts of the Enterprise Resources Market are discussed, which presents the conceptual framework of the TSCM.

In Chapter 4, the core methods of the TSCM are introduced, including the information matching algorithms and query execution methods that are critical for the operation of this model. In Chapter 5 the protocols and architecture of the TSCM, especially the exMQL, exMGQS, the Blackboard and the Export Database, are presented. In Chapter 6, the operation of the TSCM and how the components of the model interoperate to achieve the goals set out in this research are demonstrated.

In Chapter 7, the performance of the TSCM is analyzed and a discussion of the qualitative advantages of the TSCM relative to comparable research results in the field is presented. The comparison includes the MESChain system for supply chains and the RETSINA multi-agent system for general information sharing, as well as federated databases and other global database query technologies in the field. The development culminates in Chapter 8 with an overview of the research that was performed and suggestions for future work.

We might submit that chapter 7, along with Chapter 6, establishes the feasibility and correctness of the TSCM results, and thereby substantiates the claims made in the book (such as Chapter 2). More specifically, since the second stage of the TSCM is based on the Metadatabase Model, which has already been established in the literature and whose integration with the first stage is shown in the book, therefore, the correctness and promises of the first stage are what we need to prove. The analyses in Chapter 7 prove the intellectual core of the first stage: the information matching algorithms.

Chapter 2

FOUNDATIONS
Global Database Query and Market-based Resource Allocation

1. OVERVIEW

As the evolution of enterprise integration continues (see Chapter 1), the evolution of the technology for information integration continues. Scope of integration has been and will continue to be the driving force of the evolution and the determinant of the technology. The Enterprise Collaboration results developed in this book is a part of the evolution, and hence should be put in the larger context of the field of enterprise information integration. For the purpose of the research, we recognize two particular foundations based on which the TSCM results have been developed. The first is Global Database Query, of which the federated databases results are arguably the most noticeable and influential for the industry. The second is the market-based approaches to information exchange, which include a variety of results ranging from auction-oriented algorithms to agent-based market models. Among them, we focus mostly on the concepts and methods that have impacted our work and that have a direct bearing to the TSCM results from a comparison perspective. In the review of the previous results, we implicitly keep this context in mind: the integration environment that the field faces today is increasing on a global scale, perhaps numbering in the hundreds of millions of data sources. Furthermore, these global resources are owned and managed by disparate groups or individuals, with unique policies, schedules, and agendas. It is in this context that we emphasize independent databases as the target of integration.

The effort to integrate these resources manifest itself in a number of fields from a number of perspectives, which include but are not limited to grid computing and agent-oriented computing systems as well as distributed database systems. Each approach shares similar concerns: (1) how to dynamically scale the integration architecture, (2) how to dynamically include new resources, and (3) how to accommodate heterogeneous resources, both in content and physical capabilities. Although we review only the very limited subset that concerns the TSCM directly, it should still be pointed out that the larger trend in the larger literature certainly helps to solidify our concept and design.

The market-based results, including multi-agents, are reviewed first. The ensuing review on Global Query results also includes some popular Internet-motivated technologies such as Peer-to-Peer systems and Web Services.

2. MARKET-BASED MECHANISMS FOR RESOURCE MANAGEMENT AND ALLOCATION: MATCHING, AUCTION, AND AGENTS

Market-based systems, or systems that simulate a market economy, have emerged as compelling mechanisms for resource allocation. One advantage with this approach is the ability to deal with the integration complexity inherent to heterogeneous, distributed and autonomous resources. In these simulated economies, buyers represent resource consumers (e.g. applications, users) and sellers represent resource providers (e.g. database, CPU). Buyers and sellers trade resources, exchanging goods and/or services for profit. An underlying economic model, such as an auction or fixed price model facilitates the interaction between buyers and sellers. The applications of economic models for resource management are now widespread, including resource allocation and management in computing systems, manufacturing systems, communication networks, Grid computing, multi-agent systems, and distributed database management systems. Clearwater (Clearwater 1996) provides a survey of a diverse set of applications that offer market-based control of distributed resources.

In (Kwiat 2002), an illustration of the similarities between information grids and electric power grids suggests that they both offer dependable service requirements, infrastructure for large-scale pooling of resources, consistency of service, and pervasiveness. However, management issues arise due to the complexity of the resource allocation problem. It is suggested that this can be solved by creating a market and allowing prices to allocate the resources. Whereas the application of the market to the electric power grid failed (e.g. the notorious California energy crisis (Kuttner 2002; Bushnell 2004)), this was primarily due to the fact that supply was significantly less than demand, and increasing resources required expensive (time and cost) new infrastructure. On the other hand, adding more resources to the information grid is, comparatively, significantly less expensive, and so the advantage of pursuing the market model for the information grid is "appealing" (Kwiat 2002). Doing so provides for arbitrary scale, heterogeneity of resources, decentralized asynchronous operation, and tolerance of localized failures (Kwiat 2002).

A brief survey of various economic models used to manage distributed resources is provided in (Buyya, Abramson et al. 2002). Identified are: (1) the Commodity Market model, (2) Posted Price model, (3) Bargaining model, (4) Contract-Net model, and (5) Auction model among others. In the Commodity Market, consumers are charged for the amount of resources consumed. Posted price is similar to Commodity Market but services are priced to increase resource usage and influence greater consumer interest. In the Bargaining model, consumers bargain with providers on pricing and usage of the services. In Contract-Net, the consumer announces a request in the form of bid contract to which providers compete, while in an Auction, a single provider invites bids to which consumers offer bid responses. The Grid marketplace is unique in its capacity to offer these economic models across various resource management systems, which includes database systems and agent-based systems. This is demonstrated in the Nimrod-G system, a Grid resource broker that supports the commodity market, and contract-net economic models. The Nimrod-G system has the responsibility for resource discovery, resource trading, scheduling, job execution and results aggregation, and works in concert with Grid middleware to provide uniform access to Grid resources and services.

A Market-based architecture to alleviate fraud and counter-speculation that may arise in agent-to-agent negotiation is described in (Collins, Youngdahl et al. 1998; Collins, Bilot et al. 2001). The architecture combines a market, an exchange and a market session, and a series of services that are utilized across the market infrastructure.

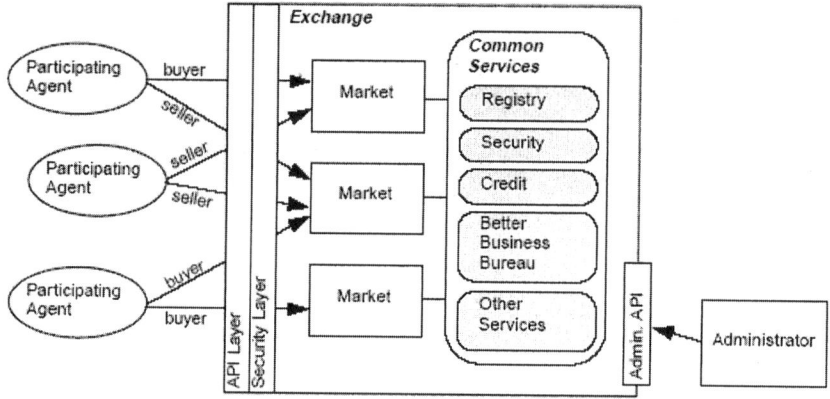

Figure 2-1. A Market Architecture for Multi-agent Contracting (Collins, Youngdahl et al. 1998)

The exchange (See Fig. 2-1) is a collection of domain specific markets in which goods and services are traded. The market facilitates trade in a specific domain, while the market-session maintains the state of agent interaction. This intermediary (the market-session) in the agent interaction provides the aforementioned controls against counter-speculation and fraud. Agents initiate bids which are submitted to the market-session. The market-session registers and timestamps the bid, and queries the registry of agents providing services. Interested agents submit responses back to the market-session which redirects the responses to the initiating client. A bid acceptance is issued to the winning bidder. The market-session enforces the rules of the market, for example, whether trade is by auction; it provides the registry of agents providing services such that no exhaustive search of the market needs to be undertaken; and, a common schema for services description. Since the market-session registers all messages in the agent interaction, it retains the state of the interaction even over periods of time. It removes the opportunity for agents to misrepresent bids, rules and timestamps essentially removing the chance for fraud and counter-speculation.

ObjectGlobe (Braumandl, Keidl et al. 2001) provides an open marketplace where queries are distributed and processed by unrelated Internet applications, although no particular economic model drives this interaction. These Internet applications are manifested as data, function and cycle providers, which can be hosted at a single site, and which offer or sell services to facilitate distributed query processing. ObjectGlobe provides a distributed, open and secure environment for query processing. A query is processed by identifying relevant providers using the ObjectGlobe lookup service, optimizing this plan according to the capabilities of the providers and user requirements, distributing the plans to the relevant providers, which will then execute the query. Security and privacy in the infrastructure are enforced by Java and popular encryption technologies, in addition to enforcing user and application policies across the distributed resources.

Computational economies have long been apart of the artificial intelligence (AI) domain, particularly multi-agent systems (MAS). The interaction of software agents in various MAS's is guided by the electronic models to facilitate interaction (Maes, Guttman et al. 1999), although other Multi-Agent Systems (MAS) (Sycara, Paolucci et al. 2003) also employ an agent communication language (ACL) that aids communication and interoperation between agents. Software agents are intelligent, autonomous and persistent and perform tasks on behalf of their owners; decision and negotiation strategies may differ from agent to agent, but the context of the interaction (or ontology) must be shared. For example, Kasbah (Maes, Guttman et al. 1999) is a multi-agent transaction system where buyer and seller agents negotiate, on behalf of their users, in a centralized marketplace. Buyer agents bid to seller agents with no restrictions on time or price, although a utility function is employed to manipulate bid amounts over time. Likewise, seller agents also benefit from utility functions in their transactions. See (Maes, Guttman et al. 1999) for a survey of agent systems. Intelligent agents also have the capability to locate themselves to more profitable areas of the market (Want, Fiddian et al. 2001). Doing so affords the agent the opportunity to increase its value in the market, while not doing so may force the removal of the agent from the market.

Manufacturing enterprises also benefit from the use of market-based control or economic models for resource management. A modified Contract-Net protocol is employed in (Heragu, Graves et al. 2002) as the negotiation protocol for real-time task/job allocation. Intelligent agents representing manufacturing systems and manufacturing components bid and negotiate for jobs. The price set for jobs depend on multiple factors including required processing time (e.g., processing time required for a part), the utilization of resources (e.g., a material handling device), whether or not the resource is already committed, as well as system-wide factors.

Business-to-Business (B2B) commerce has been largely aided by large private trading exchanges, e.g, CommerceOne (CommerceOne 2006). These are companies that provide a framework to facilitate interoperability between businesses. The framework may contain a catalog of services offered by participating companies, a unified view of products that can be traded, as well as automated trading mechanisms (Sairamesh, Mohan et al. 2002). The exchanges are largely aided by standards (Sundaram and Shim

26

2001; Tsalgatidou and Pilioura 2002) that define a common framework to which all participating members must subscribe, in order to facilitate trade.

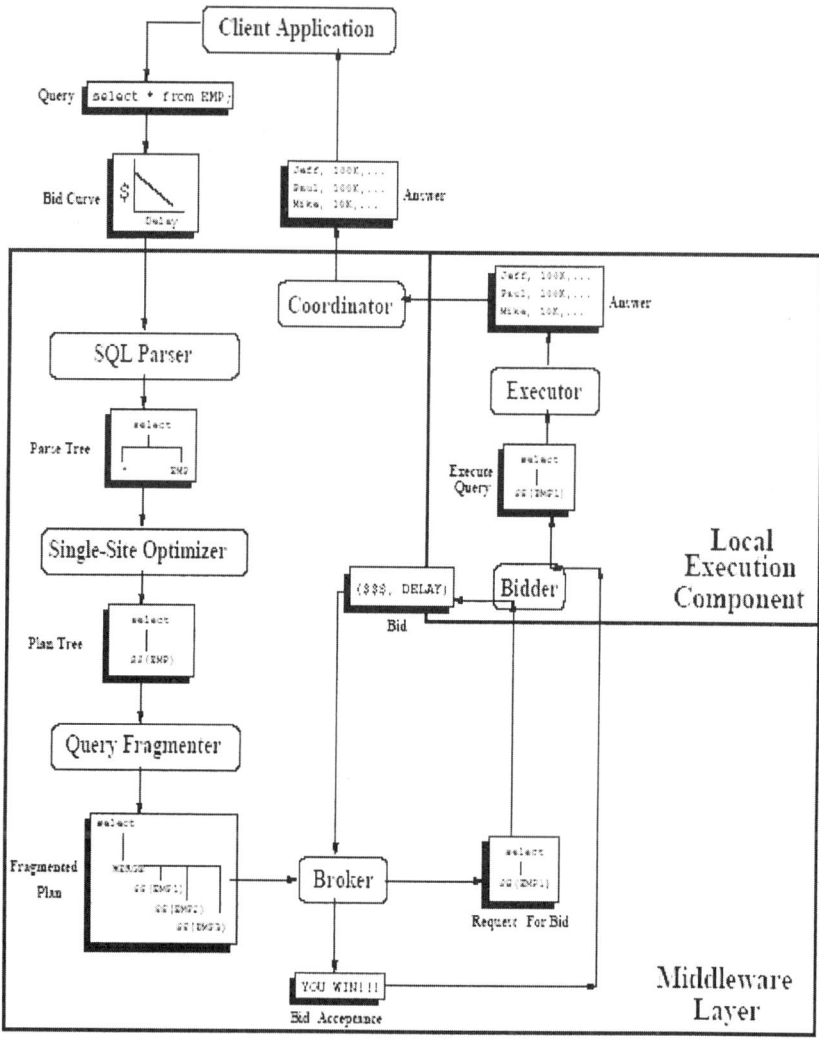

Figure 2-2. The Mariposa Architecture (Stonebraker, Aoki et al. 1996)

Mariposa (Stonebraker, Aoki et al. 1996) is a market-based wide-area distributed database management system (See Fig. 2-2). A primary problem of the distributed database management approach has been the complexity of integrating databases distributed over wide-area networks.

The market-based approach reduces the complexity to a function of price and time. Cooperating databases bid in this framework to process queries initiated by a client application. Each database possesses a client application that enables the construction of queries, a middleware layer that performs query preparation and brokering capabilities, and a local execution component that responds to and executes bids and queries respectively. At the core of the framework is the concept of budgets. When a query is submitted by the client application, a budget represented as a non-increasing function of time, is allocated to the query that represents the value of the query to the client, that is, the amount that will be paid for the query to be answered in a specified amount of time. The query and the budget are both submitted to the Mariposa middleware layer, where it is processed. The resulting query plans (which may be decomposed into multiple queries plans) are passed on to the broker, which sends out bids to other Mariposa sites (the bids consist of the query along with the budget). The bidding process is facilitated by an advertising system consisting of name servers that store advertisements from cooperating databases. These databases post advertisements describing the services offered and brokers read the advertisements to locate databases willing to execute the bid.

Mariposa utilizes two economic models as the underlying bid protocol, (1) expensive bid, and (2) purchase order. In the expensive bid protocol, the broker first submits the bid request to other Mariposa sites. Interested bidders respond to the broker with a bid that defines the cost for processing, the expiration date of the bid and the delay to start processing the bid. The broker assembles all bid responses, chooses the winning bid and notifies the winning bidder of acceptance. It may or may not inform the losing bidders. The purchase order protocol is "cheaper" than the expensive bid due to the lower number of messages required in the bidding process. Here the broker submits queries to other Mariposa sites without an expectation that the bid will be processed, and without knowledge of the costs and delay of the service. Capable and interested bidders process the query and return the results, along with a bill for services.

The term *matchmaking* is used within the multi-agent systems domain to define the entire agent interaction process, from the match on search terms, to negotiation and then agreement.

The matchmaking process in (Sim and Chan 2000; Sim and Wong 2001) involves the comparison of requests from buyers with advertisements from sellers that are stored in a Blackboard database. A broker agent is responsible for identifying matches between requests and advertisements, which are represented by multi-attribute sets. The matching algorithm is enabled by a series of conditional loops that compare the attributes of the requests and advertisements. (Sycara, Lu et al. 1999) on the other hand utilizes an agent capability description language called LARKS (Language for Advertisement and Request for Knowledge-Sharing) to describe the requests and advertisements of agents. LARKS supports multiple stages of matching (or filtering, as described in the (Sycara, Lu et al. 1999)) that span context matching, similarity matching and constraint matching among others. The matchmaking process qualifies the type of match; it is an exact match, plug-in match or relaxed match, where each type of match is derived from various combinations of the aforementioned filters.

In (Rahwan, Kowalczyk et al. 2002; Kurbel and Loutchko 2003) the authors delineate between concerns that arise in multi-player negotiations, such as, one-to-one, one-to-many, and many-to-many agent interactions. One-to-many and many-to-many interactions are realized through the use of a coordinating agent that manages (coordinates) the individual one-to-one agent negotiations (Rahwan, Kowalczyk et al. 2002). Many-to-many negotiations are achieved by the negotiation of multiple one-to-many interactions (Kurbel and Loutchko 2003).

In (Di Noia, Di Sciascio et al. 2000) the authors deviate from negotiation and focus on the search process and the evaluation (ranking) of matches. They offer two interesting properties of the matchmaking process; first, the absence of information in a demand or supply should imply opportunity for refinement rather than rejection. Second, depending on the perspective taken in the matchmaking process, different evaluations may arise. If a supply appears to be a subset of a demand, then it would rank highly as a match, whereas the converse may not be true.

3.   GLOBAL QUERY SYSTEMS

Traditional Global Query methods require varying degrees of control over participating databases, for example, a specific query language must be shared, or a common data model is necessary to integrate large numbers of databases. The following literature review explores data integration in three particular areas, Global Query Systems which is further classified as Federated Database Systems and other Multidatabase approaches, Global Schema Integration, and Multidatabase Languages. The review culminates in a comparative analysis of the related literature with the Two-Stage Collaboration Model (TSCM).

Global Schema Integration methods (Batini, Lenzerini et al. 1986; Beynon-Davies, Bonde et al. 1997; Rahm and Bernstein 2001) consolidate the schemas of multiple distributed databases into a single global schema, which avails the enterprise user with a unified view of enterprise data, providing system transparency (the user need not be knowledgeable about system configuration), in addition to resolving semantic conflicts that may exist among the multiple systems. Federated Database Systems (FDSs) (Sheth and Larson 1990) provide greater autonomy for local systems, although a global schema may still be employed for data integration. Whereas a single global schema is required for data integration in the aforementioned global schema approach, multiple schemas are allowed in the federated approach. These multiple schemas vary by control and complexity, for example, a global federation administrator can define a global schema, through which all federated databases interact (single controller, high complexity), or local administrators can define their own integrated schemas (multiple controllers, low complexity). Multidatabase Languages (Litwin 1985) are applied to pre-existing heterogeneous database environments that lack a global controller or integrated schema. No integration measures are taken to consolidate the distributed databases; rather, the multidatabase language incorporates the necessary constructs to query the participating databases. In Multidatabase Languages, knowledge of the overall database environment is necessary for operation, such that, users must know where specific data reside in order to perform, joins or scans on database relations, and so on.

These three aforementioned methods differ in the autonomy and heterogeneity of the participant distributed databases, which subsequently affect the scalability of the integration environment. Sheth and Larson (Sheth and Larson 1990) classify databases with respect to autonomy, which includes: (1) Design, (2) Communication, (3) Execution, and (4) Association autonomy. Heterogeneity in distributed databases systems may arise as a result of either differences in hardware, software or communication capabilities; or differences in data semantics. (See (Sheth and Larson 1990) for further details on this subject). For the purposes of this research, scalability pertains to the ability of the data integration solution to add increasingly large numbers of databases without compromising functionality and performance, but rather embracing full advantage of the available resources. Kossmann (Kossmann 2000) provides a survey of the recent developments in query processing architectures.

Garlic (Carey, Haas et al. 1995; Haas, Miller et al. 1999) provides the integration and management of heterogeneous multimedia information repositories, using an object-oriented modeling paradigm. Multimedia data include text, images, CAD drawings, and medical objects. The Garlic architecture consists of data repositories which are independent of the centralized controller, and are integrated into the Garlic framework via wrappers that perform query and data transformations (See Fig. 2-3). Each wrapper translates information about the schemas and queries between

Garlic internal protocols and the repositories native protocols. Query processing is provided by the Query Services and Runtime System components which avails applications and end users with a unified schema of the Garlic database through which queries, updates and method invocation requests are issued. Queries are expressed in an object-oriented extension to the SQL query language. The Garlic query browser provides the end user with a graphical interface that supports interactive browsing, navigation and querying of the Garlic databases.

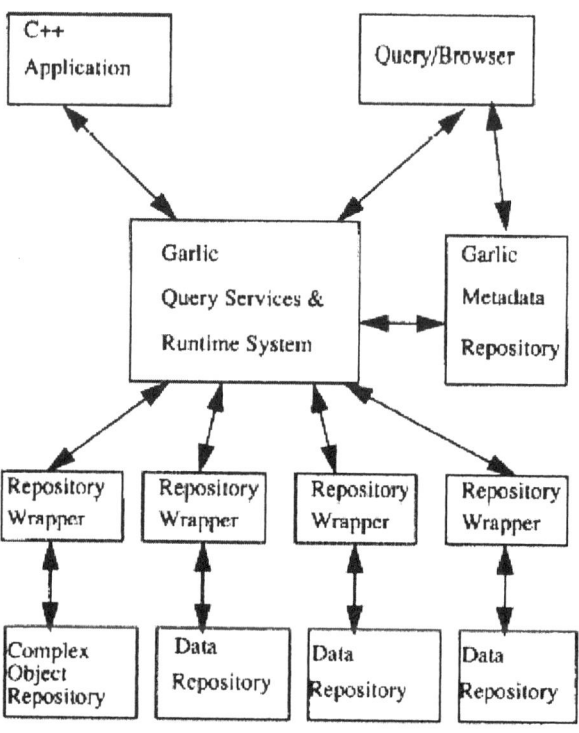

Figure 2-3. Garlic Architecture (Carey, Haas et al. 1995)

The IBM DB2 (Haas, Lin et al. 2002) architecture is rooted in Garlic mentioned above, and integrates federated data sources with user defined functions and wrappers. The simplest approaches to data integration in DB2 is the scalar User-Defined Function (UDF) that returns a scalar result, and the table UDF, which returns a table as output. The third and most powerful is the wrapper, which allows the complete integration of a federated data source. The wrapper is the mediator between the data source and DB2, and maps the source data model to the DB2 data model while also transforming operations on DB2 to operations at the source. DB2 facilitates system transparency, heterogeneity, extensibility and autonomy. The underlying "idiosyncrasies and implementations" are hidden from the user, which arise due to the variety in the data source, i.e. hardware and software, and so on. New data sources can be dynamically added, and the functionality of the data source is not compromised by its addition to the federation.

InfoSleuth (Bayardo, Bohrer et al. 1997) resembles a market-based system with its use of cooperating agents within an open and dynamic architecture, but the absence of a computational economy disqualifies it as such. The heterogeneity of data sources on the World Wide Web and the inability to access information based on semantic "concepts" in this environment are the primary concerns of the InfoSleuth project. Accordingly, agent technologies and domain ontologies are employed to facilitate information brokering in a dynamic and open environment. The InfoSleuth architecture consists of cooperating agents that represent information resources, from users to databases, communicating via Knowledge Query and Manipulation Language (KQML) (Finin, Fritzson et al. 1994), which encapsulates queries and requests represented in SQL and Knowledge Interchange Format (KIF), respectively. User agents represent users, which interact with the network of agents via a Java applet. The user agent facilitates the formulation of queries using domain ontologies, and presents the user with the results. Other agents in the network, including ontology, broker, resource, task execution, and others, all interact to support the interoperation of distributed data and services. In particular, the ontology agent serves as the overall knowledge base of ontologies, providing all agents in the architecture with an agreed upon terminology of agent contexts as well as the ontology for the information handled by agents.

The Observer system (Mena, Illarramendi et al. 2000) is concerned with the loss of semantic information when a query is translated from one domain to another. Accordingly, Observer's *vocabulary sharing* translates queries into a target ontologies given pre-defined mappings defined in an inter-ontology relationship manager. Observer accounts for inexact matches in the translation of queries from one domain to another; regarded as partial translation, by measuring the loss of information given alternative translations and chooses the one with the least loss of information.

The Carnot project (Collet, Huhns et al. 1991; Singh, Cannata et al. 1997) utilizes the Cyc knowledge base as the basis of a global schema (Lenat 1995) to facilitate resource integration. Resource integration is achieved by translating individual resource schemas to the global schema via *articulation axioms* that describe the equivalence between components of different domains. Consequently, queries issued at an individual resource are first translated into the global context language (GCL), both semantically and syntactically, and then to the local database manipulation languages. These queries can also be issued against the global view which is then distributed to the individual resources, although this requires knowledge of the GCL. The Carnot approach avoids the traditional global schema management problem by merging individual schemas with the global schema, as opposed to with each other. This not only retains the integrity of individual and global schemas, but provides for simpler construction and management of the global schema.

Pegasus (Ahmed, DeSmedt et al. 1991; Ahmed, Albert et al. 1993) is a heterogeneous, multidatabase management system, based on the object-oriented data modeling paradigm, that provides native access to heterogeneous and autonomous databases, and database management systems. The data abstraction and encapsulation facilities of the object-oriented paradigm, creates an extensible framework for dealing with the heterogeneities common in traditional database systems.

Query processing is made more efficient by deploying necessary application functionality (for example, query operators) to remote sites, as opposed to consolidating and processing data at a global site. MOCHA (Rodríguez-Martínez and Roussopoulos 2000) is database middleware, developed in JAVA, that provides such functionality. In traditional systems, tremendous effort would be undertaken to deploy the operators throughout the distributed computer network, or to interconnect multiple data sites, due to heterogeneities that may exist in the hardware and software, as well as the overhead realized in data shipping and query shipping. MOCHA deploys JAVA code dynamically to remote sites, dubbed *code shipping*, resulting in improved and efficient query optimization and subsequently reduced query execution times. The Query Processing Coordinator (QPC) provides the query processing functionality and deploys all necessary application functionality to clients and remote sites. The Data Access Provider interfaces with the data sources, providing an execution engine that processes the specific application functionality, and so differs from wrappers found in traditional systems.

The MDV system (Keidl, Kreutz et al. 2002) is a distributed metadatabase management systems that speeds up access to distributed data sources by replicating and caching metadata about participating resources and services in the middle-tier of its three-tier architecture. The architecture is comprised of Metadata Providers (MDP), Local Metadata Repositories (LMR) and MDV clients. MDP's synchronize metadata amongst themselves to provide uniform access to metadata by LMR's; while LMR's cache and replicate metadata relevant to local users and applications (MDV clients), using a publish and subscribe algorithm.

4.   EMERGING INTEGRATION TECHNOLOGIES: WEB SERVICES, P2P AND THE SEMANTIC WEB

Peer-to-Peer (P2P) networks and Web Services are emerging as *de facto* standards for data integration and information sharing. Data providers and consumers participate in *ad-hoc* data sharing arrangements on their own terms, in real-time, and on-demand. These technologies are inherently scalable and heterogeneous; however the data sources are partially autonomous as the data providers typically must subscribe to some global information sharing standard or proprietary data format of a facilitating application.   It is also important to note that these technologies are applications that sit a layer above data sources, not core technologies such as databases and query languages, such that the data sources or database facilitate data sharing but are typically passive functions of the application.

4.1   Web Services

Business Process Management (Dayal, Hsu et al. 2001) provides for the automation and integration of business processes, and is presently manifested as a system of Web Services, that foster a services-oriented paradigm.   As described in (Fremantle, Weerawarana et al. 2002; Tsalgatidou and Pilioura 2002), the underlying Web Services technology include SOAP, UDDI, WSDL and WSIL. SOAP, Simple Object Access Protocol, provides messaging capabilities; while UDDI, Universal Description, Discovery and Integration protocol, provides directory or lookup services, which categorize businesses according to industry and so on. WSIL, Web Services Inspection Language, provides the method to determine what services are located at a particular site; and WSDL, Web Services Description Language, offers the ability to describe a Web Service. The attractive feature of the BPM approach is software and applications can be componentized and deployed as Web Services, without disruption of their original functionality. Furthermore, any application or data source can be deployed as a Web Service as long as they can be described using the open and standards based WSDL and its associated technologies.

4.2   Peer-to-Peer Networks

In P2P networks, individual nodes connecting to the Internet can access real-time index of files shared by other active nodes (Parameswaran, Susarla et al. 2001).   P2P networks provide various advantages, most importantly, improved search capabilities relative to web-based search engines. Here, data shared is current, since the node refreshes its content whenever connected to the network. Load balancing, redundancy and fault tolerance, though typically found in more advanced P2P implementations, are additional benefits of the P2P architecture, such that content is distributed throughout the network, and most likely will not be lost if parts of the network were to fail. However, the downsides of P2P include *noise* in resulting query results since there is no standard to describe shared resources, as well as the semantic heterogeneities that will arise due to individual naming conventions and content representation.

JXTA on the other hand, is a suite of protocols that facilitate P2P communication (Waterhouse, Doolin et al. 2002). The protocols are XML-derived, which provides platform independence and network transparency. JXTA peers can exist as providers and consumers as well as hubs that redirect query requests to other peers.

Freenet (Clarke, Miller et al. 2002) is a self-organizing and decentralized P2P global information storage system, which promotes the autonomy of system participants. It provides stability and fault tolerance by automatically replicating and relocating files according to user demand.

4.3   The Semantic Web

As the World Wide Web continues to evolve, it is necessary for information providers to describe their content with terms that are universally shared. Hendler (Hendler 2001) posits that ontologies fill this need by providing a set of terms, including a vocabulary and simple rules of inference and logic, for some particular topic such as shopping for pets. In these situations, information providers define and markup content in terms derived from a central ontology, such as the DARPA Agent Markup Language (DAML) (McIlraith, Son et al. 2001). The nature of ontologies however, allows them to be extended such that information providers can create a derived ontology which can in turn be used by other providers. The challenge therefore to achieve widespread use of ontologies, is to develop tools to simplify these procedures for the average user, and make it trivial to create semantically defined content.

4.4   XML

XML (W3C 2004) provides the foundation for a number of the nascent technologies used for data integration and sharing. The ubiquity of XML stems from its acceptance as an open standard, and the simplicity with which XML content can be created and exchanged between heterogeneous systems. XQuery (Chamberlin 2002) provides the opportunity to query an XML document, akin to SQL and relational databases. Associated technologies, XML Path Language (XPath) (W3C 2004), Extensible Stylesheet Language Transformations (XSLT) (W3C 2004) facilitate the selection of elements in an XML document as well as the transformation of XML documents from one format to another, respectively.

5.   METADATABASE AND ROPE

The Metadatabase project at Rensselaer Polytechnic Institute explores information integration in the enterprise. The results, after a decade of research, include the Metadatabase – an information resource management system for distributed, autonomous and heterogeneous environments; and ROPE – a programming environment that extends the interoperability and adaptiveness of the Metadatabase, through the use of extensible software shells.

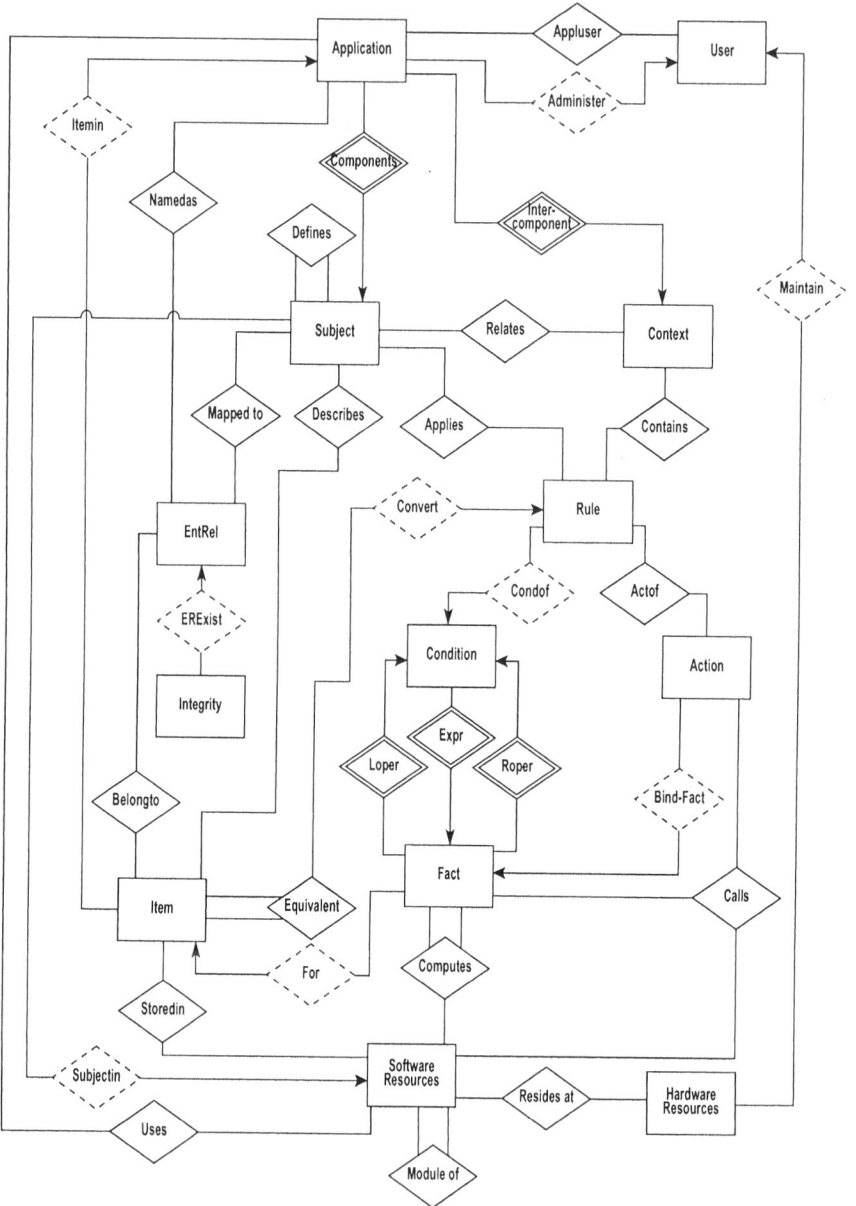

Figure 2-4. Global Information Resources Dictionary (GIRD)

The role of traditional distributed systems has been to integrate distributed data sources, without regard for the context in which the data is used. Conversely, the Metadatabase approaches this integration problem from a holistic perspective, that is, how the applications / systems / databases interact and contribute to intra-enterprise synergies. This is regarded as enterprise intelligence, or enterprise knowledge, expressed in the form of business rules which include triggers, integrity constraints, and decision knowledge that describe information workflows between applications / systems / databases; as well as, control knowledge that delineate global equivalence knowledge and data transfer rules between the information resources. This enterprise knowledge is metadata, and is regarded as the basis of database integration in the Metadatabase architecture.

5.1 Two Stage Entity Relationship Method (TSER)

The Metadatabase architecture is comprised of three elements, a conceptual model of the enterprise, which includes all knowledge and information resources; a physical representation method that any capable relational database management system (RDBMS) can provide; and the Metadatabase management system, a management framework that provides query and metadata management and modeling facilities. The first element, the conceptual model, is manifested in the Global Information Resources Dictionary (GIRD) (See Fig. 2-4), a unified representational model of enterprise metadata. The GIRD model is created using the Two-Stage Entity-Relationship (TSER) approach (Hsu, Bouziane et al. 1991; Hsu, Tao et al. 1993; Hsu 1996), a modeling methodology that provides a representation method for the contextual knowledge of the enterprise as well as its data objects. TSER encompasses a multi-stage modeling methodology that begins with the system analysis and representation of the application / information system / user level (or functional layer). Two constructs are used to model this functional layer, SUBJECTS which describe the data objects and CONTEXT which is used to describe the intended context of the data objects. The functional layer is recursively decomposed, to produce additional functional views representing components of the enterprise information system. Dependency theory-based algorithms are then applied to the completed functional model to map the functional layer to a normalized structural model – described using four general constructs, ENTITY (OE) and three classes of integrity RELATIONSHIPs: functional (FR), plural (PR) and mandatory (MR) – which guarantees the model to be at least in third normal form. A subsequent phase of the TSER methodology generates an import schema that is amenable to input into an RDBMS (See (Hsu, Bouziane et al. 1991; Hsu, Tao et al. 1993; Hsu 1996) for a complete description of the TSER approach).

5.2   Metadatabase Management System (MDBMS)

The Metadatabase Management System (Bouziane 1991) provides basic metadata management capabilities, that is, insert, delete, update and retrieve similar to traditional relational database manipulation language constructs, however, these actions are performed on metadata. An additional management tool provided by the MDBMS is the Model-Assisted Global Query System (MGQS) (Cheung and Hsu 1996) that provides syntax-free online assistance for query formulation and processing, supports local autonomy, local system transparency and local systems interoperation. Users interact with MGQS through a graphical user interface (GUI) that accommodates model traversal and subsequent query formulation. The user selects metadata items relevant to his/her interest or perspective, which may correspond with application, functional, structural views, or actual metadata items, and MGQS produces a completely formulated and optimized global query (additional metadata items, if necessary, are included by the system – hence online assistance). Global query formulation capabilities are provided by the non-procedural Metadatabase Query Language (MQL) (Cheung and Hsu 1996), a global query language that supports queries across distributed and heterogeneous local systems with different schemata as well as different data semantics.

As is, the Metadatabase is a stand-alone, semi-active knowledge-base. The global system administrator creates a global data model using the individual schemata of the distributed applications using the TSER methodologies mentioned earlier. Global queries can then be executed against the Metadatabase via MQGS or MQL (Cheung and Hsu 1996) from the global or local perspective. Local users within the enterprise interact directly with the Metadatabase, or through an interface deployed at the local application site. It is important to note that users of the Metadatabase need not be knowledgeable about the underlying distributed architecture; the Metadatabase avails the enterprise user of full system transparency. Global queries are decomposed and transformed into the local query format by the global query processor and translator of the MGQS. Local queries are sent to the relevant local applications via the communication network and executed at the local application. Local results are returned to the MGQS, merged into a global result by the result integrator of the MGQS, and then presented to the enterprise user (Hsu, Babin et al. 1992).

5.3   ROPE

ROPE (Babin 1993) transforms the Metadatabase into an active and adaptive integration architecture. Here, the operating and decision rules are instead located at the local sites, and reside there, as opposed to being completely referenced in the Metadatabase architecture. This adds the functionality for local sites to actively respond to rule-based changes in the local architecture, without consideration of the Metadatabase (hence, an increase in local autonomy). Thus, if changes to the local application takes place, through temporal or event-based triggers, and these changes affect the global architecture (the Metadatabase and other local sites) then ROPE provides the functionality to distribute these changes. This is facilitated by software shells that surround, and enhance the functionality of the local applications (Hsu and Babin 1993). The software shells are identical for all local applications; however, the knowledge possessed by the shells (represented as operating rules) are tailored to each application. ROPE is a programming environment that defines (1) how the software are created, (2) how the shells behave, and (3) how the shells are managed (Hsu and Babin 1993). It also integrates with the Metadatabase to push rule-based changes from the Metadatabase, downstream to the local applications, and for the local applications to push new knowledge upstream to the Metadatabase, or across to other local applications.

6.   A COMPARATIVE ANALYSIS OF THE TWO-STAGE COLLABORATION MODEL WITH THE RELATED LITERATURE

A critical and required feature required of collaboration on the Internet is the resolution of semantic and structural heterogeneities that exist as a result of heterogeneous data models. The proposed Two-Stage Collaboration Model (TSCM) offers a solution for semantic heterogeneity in the global equivalence feature of the TSER modeling methodology (See Chapter 5). Semantically equivalent data items or objects that exist throughout the enterprise, in the disparate data models are made equivalent to each other during the TSER modeling process. An item with the same semantics, which is determined by the designer, is "mapped" to the global model, such that queries against the Metadatabase or a participating local database will retrieve the variants of the data items and present these in global query results. On the contrary, the Carnot project (Collet, Huhns et al. 1991) maps local data models to the CYC knowledge-base, but the scalability of this architecture is limited, as it is a manual effort to define the knowledge-base. Also, various other integration architectures, for example, Mariposa (Stonebraker, Aoki et al. 1996) and ObjectGlobe (Braumandl, Keidl et al. 2001) assume homogeneous semantics, where participant databases speak the same language and data items and objects share the same meaning throughout the integration framework. Ontologies (Hendler 2001) offer improved classification of data semantics; however, the rigorous modeling and representation method of the Metadatabase supersedes any offering currently provided in this area.

Structural heterogeneities are addressed using the TSER modeling process (See Chapter 5). Relational, object-oriented, and object-relational databases represent a sample of the data models that can be modeled using TSER methodologies. Each data model is first represented using TSER functional constructs, then structural constructs, and then finally transformed into a comprehensive physical model corresponding to the relational paradigm. The process is repeated for each database to be integrated into the global data model. Conversely, for new databases to be added to Garlic (Carey, Haas et al. 1995) and DB2 (Haas, Lin et al. 2002) a wrapper must be created, and extensive work is required if the data model is entirely new. In Pegasus (Ahmed, DeSmedt et al. 1991; Ahmed, Albert et al. 1993), an import schema is generated for each external database, which span object, relational, and hierarchical data models – although the complexity of importation increases moving from object to hierarchical – and these are imported into the Pegasus schema to form a unified schema. Agent-based systems such as InfoSleuth (Bayardo, Bohrer et al. 1997) address semantic and structural heterogeneities in ontologies and agent modeling respectively. Typically, the agent architecture is homogeneous, with respect to architecture, such that integration across heterogeneous agent architectures requires manual intervention to resolve differences between agent communication languages, and so on.

Market-based systems in general, address the traditional global query problem with respect to integration scalability, given various degrees of database autonomy and heterogeneity, by regarding the member databases as buyers and sellers of information that trade resources for financial benefit. This approach offers numerous advantages: because of the market paradigm, member databases are not tied to a specific architecture and are free to join and disjoin the integration. Moreover, the integration and global query can span increasingly greater numbers of databases than that found in traditional approaches to database integration and global query. In fact, the scalability of traditional distributed database management systems are compromised by the optimization phase (Özsu and Valduriez 1991) of the query processor. Traditional approaches (Ribeiro, Ribeiro et al. 1997) generate query execution plans through algorithmic searches or heuristics, and measure these based on various costs: inter-site communications/network cost, response times, CPU and I/O costs. Consequently, as the search space grows (that is, the number of databases participating in the integration increases to a very large number), then the evaluation becomes exponentially complex or intractable. ObjectGlobe (Braumandl, Keidl et al. 2001) employs a lookup service to identify unrelated data sources, query operators and servers on which to execute a query, but, the resources must register beforehand to participate in query operations. ObjectGlobe also requires that query operators be created using JAVA, which compromises heterogeneity within the architecture.

Chapter 3

A GENERAL MODEL
Enterprise Resources Market

1. OVERVIEW

This chapter is drawn from (Hsu 2002; Hsu and Carothers 2003; Hsu and Carothers 2004; Hsu, Carothers, and Levermore 2006), and highlights the general concepts from which the design of the Two-Stage Collaboration Model is derived. Intellectually, the ERM model is a general conceptual design that the Two-Stage Collaboration Model substantiates through a particular new method: information matching, which in its own right is a major and self-contained result in the field. We discuss the ERM model here both as a conceptual design for the general problem of integration of information resources (databases, files, computing resources, and others) in single or multiple enterprises, and as a conceptual basis for the TSCM results. We establish first the general problem and discuss the ERM model from this perspective.

Research has shown that market-style self-scheduling is a promising approach to resolving the problem of real-time online resources allocation. However, previous results tend to focus on manufacturing and other physical systems that lack some of the challenges of today's extended information enterprises. When the real-time products and processes span multiple organizations at different parts of the world, the complexity of data semantics and performance requirements could violate some of the basic assumptions of previous models. Yet, this level of resource sharing is a key to new Internet-centric computing visions as well as enterprise integration.

2.   MARKET-STYLE SELF-SCHEDULING

Information enterprises include virtual enterprises, extended enterprises, and enterprises that feature information production and integration. For the purpose of this paper, they feature conspicuously the use of Internet technology to reach out and integrate, and thereby improve their performance. The intelligence community, news organizations, the ASP (Application Service Provider) model of e-business, industrial exchanges (e.g., Covisint, FreeMarkets, and CommerceOne), and the service business of industrial equipment manufacturers (e.g., Boeing and GE Industrial Systems) are representative examples. At the heart of these enterprises is the scheduling and control of their resources - i.e., the databases, networked computers, and the like; which tend to be widely distributed and heterogeneous in their technical design, and may also require openness and scalability of the regimes that inter-operate with them. Without enterprise-wide management of these resources, an information enterprise cannot operate at high level of integration and hence can hardly capture the full benefits of extended enterprising. However, resource allocation for (Internet-based) information enterprises can be more involved to design than the scheduling regimes for traditional enterprises such as manufacturing and transportation, because of the nature of information production. In fact, this can be characterized as a resource allocation problem under the conditions of globally distributed resources and users (providers and requesters), heterogeneous information models, and real-time assignment with online performance measurement and adjustment. In this paper it is referred to as the enterprise resource allocation problem.

The enterprise resource allocation problem defies many premises of classical scheduling theory (Conway, Maxwell et al. 1967) and online scheduling (Hochbaum and Shmoys 1987; Coppersmith and Raghavan 1989). The classical paradigm focuses on optimizing the supply (resources) with respect to a given demand (tasks), subject to workflow precedence and other job constraints. This leads to the dichotomy of resource versus user in the tradition of manufacturing, where machines and jobs are two orthogonal genres and it does not consider the possibility that a job could be a resource, nor a resource a job. Therefore, the instances of each genre are homogeneous in their technical nature; and both genres can be characterized in a unified set of definitive terms such as machining capacity, classes or functions, and processing times. The matching of a job to a machine in this context is never ambiguous and the objective function can be neatly analyzed with respect to throughput, make-span, tardiness, utilization rate, and other physical performance measures. When necessary, such as in online scheduling for computers, an assignment can even be moved around as in bin packing, in order to optimize the overall performance within a single migration round. Finally, a scheduling regime is designed to be a planner rather than an executioner, and it does not consider real-time conditions nor online feedback from the system that executes the schedules when it determines the schedules. The literature assumes that either the system's controller will adjust the schedules to accommodate real time conditions, or the scheduler will re-run itself with new conditions to produce a new result in the next planning window.

For Internet information enterprises, the resource allocation regime would have to do better since the environment includes not only physical facilities but also information resources such as databases and personal information assets. The regime must produce maximum quantity of information to maximum suitable users with maximum relevance and quality, with minimum delay. Thus, the regime has to encourage information sharing, respond to real-time conditions online, and re-allocate resources according to performance feedback. That is, it must consider both the supply and the demand. The regime must allow for resources providers to also be users; e.g., a field officer could both provide and request information and an automated analysis system or a database might request input or even co-processing from other facilities as well as produce output. In addition, these providing or requesting tasks might use different data semantics to describe their information contents and requirements. When information exchange is involved, the semantic uniqueness makes tasks heterogeneous and requiring individual, custom representation, attention, and processing. Furthermore, Internet information enterprises involve extended organization (inter-organizational tasks), globally distributed resources and users, and potentially, very large number of participants. These characteristics fit best with those of an artificial market, such as a stock exchange or industrial exchange in e-business.

A number of researchers have recently proposed market-style resource allocation schemes using software agents to make conventional scheduling models more in line with real-time assignment (Baker 1998; Swaminathan, Smith et al. 1998; Cesta, Oddi et al. 2000; Nandula and Dutta 2000; Prabhu 2000; Parunak 2001; Heragu, Graves et al. 2002). These newer efforts tend to create a pseudo market, for example, shop floor scheduling and computer networks allocation, where facility agents and job agents meet and match. These works, however, tend to lack an effective market mechanism - i.e., a performance-feedback-reward loop - to measure the value of the resources in the market and thereby approach global optimality. Without this self-correcting capability, the pseudo market is more a metaphor than a complete mechanism capable of capturing the benefits of the market model. These designs also tend to ignore the adaptive capacity of agents required to perform semantics matching, multi-criteria negotiation, and other dynamic tasks. They do not consider how to create efficiently large number of agents online and effectively manage these agents when updates are necessary, either. These issues become critical when the pseudo market were to scale up to handling, say, hundreds or even millions of concurrent, custom tasks. Consequently, the assignment schemes developed in the previous designs do not offer sufficient feedback and adaptation to assure self-correction. Not surprisingly, some of these pseudo markets exhibit various global inefficiencies (e.g., long queues at certain resources sites caused by obsolete information at the global site, and tasks not getting assigned properly due to lack of negotiation); and others excessive overhead (imposition of a global controller to supersede the self-scheduling. All of them lack the promises to address the potential of influencing demand and supply such as encouraging information sharing.

In contrast, a full-fledged artificial market model is developed, the Enterprise Resources Market, as a solution to the enterprise resource allocation problem. The solution uses the proven technology of industrial exchanges and new results developed in the research to accomplish self-scheduling with the balance of demand and supply, computational efficiency (linear to low polynomial complexity), information interchange (semantics match), and self-correction (performance feedback and reward) for Internet information enterprises. The model extends the previous exchanges from focusing on information tasks to allocating both physical and information resources that the enterprises involve, and from relying on a global Blackboard to allow execution of the information processing tasks at the local level on a peer-to-peer basis. Collectively, the new results provide an agent model and an agent-based architecture to connect distributed resource providers and users to the market, as well as directly to each other. The new agent model allows for very large number of concurrent participants (exponentially scalable) to use software surrogates to globally publish their offers and requests of resources, and match-negotiate-auction (at a global Blackboard); and then connect locally with their matches to subscribe to the resources. It also provides an alternative peer-to-peer negotiation model to allow matching and auction among local sites without a global Blackboard. A pricing model drives negotiation and feedback towards achieving a globally sound, self-scheduling regime. The pricing model encourages sharing of information and resources in the same time it controls the use of them. In this regime, both providers and users can initiate tasks as bids for transaction, while a global server facilitates the creation, management, and processing of their custom (task-oriented) agents. The global server uses metadata technology to represent task characteristics, including transaction requirements and data semantics, and to match requests with offerings according to these characteristics. It subsequently conducts the negotiation, auction, and final connection of tasks to local resources. As such, the objective function is the maximization of the total (perceived) value of information and physical resources. It is worthwhile to note that the pricing model gives rise to a market mechanism that encompasses and synthesizes such criteria as minimization of delay in assignment and optimal utilization of resources, as well as provides performance-based rewards and adjustment, in a way similar to that associated with a natural market. The constraints are the transaction requirements and data semantics of tasks, which could be updated real-time and online through the task agents, based on local conditions (e.g., work load and deadline). Self-scheduling takes place at matching, the allocation-connection, and the queuing at the local resources; and hence assure computational efficiency. Finally, note that the Enterprise Resources Market accomplishes both resource allocation and information sharing for the extended organization. With the pricing model, it optimally allocates the published tasks and helps subscribe to the resources; without it, it still matches tasks and helps interchange of information resources.

In summary, the self-scheduling resource allocation model is motivated by extended information enterprises and solves a problem formulated with a clear logical objective function and constraints. Its new results contribute to the agent technology and distributed computing, as well as the field of exchanges of e-business. In the next section we discuss how this Enterprise Resources Market works; whose design and attendant new results are then presented in Section 4.

3.   THE AGENT-BASED, PEER-TO-PEER PUBLISH AND SUBSCRIBE MODEL

We define that the user community, i.e. the organizations involved, encompasses multiple operating groups, databases and computing networks all of whom have information and can process data. Both the human and machine components of the community can both be providers and requesters of information resources. That is, all participants of the market can play both roles of sellers and buyers (e.g., an automated information system may trigger a request for information or co-processing from other sources during the execution of an analysis). The organization uses budgets to control the allocation and utilization of information resources. All users, therefore, pay from their funds (real money or fungible credit) for their requesting tasks (buy) and take revenue from their offering tasks (sell). The market is, hence, a performance and reward mechanism, as well; to which the management could complement additional adjustments of funding, as desired.

Participants use task-oriented and manageable agents to publish their requests and offers of resources, and use the same to subscribe to the resources. Software agents bring about several significant advantages: asynchronous (24/7) transaction, controllable consistency with enterprise knowledge and requirements, and security (e.g., the participant can publish only the information slated to offer, and conceal the true nature of the tasks or identity of the requesters from the providers if necessary). The design of the agents must also include additional intelligence such as preferences and transaction rules to further automate negotiation and peer-to-peer transaction as described below.

At the global server level, a blackboard is maintained to match requests and offers based on task characteristics such as deadline, specific requirements, availability, and perceived value in terms of price. The criteria allow for non-exact or staggered match. After one or more matches are found, a pricing model will perform the assignment, which entails negotiation, including group auction and revision of terms, amongst the matched parties if alternative allocations exist. The global server maintains and makes available the market status to all participants to help them publish their bids and negotiate, as well as provide remedy to tasks having difficulty getting allocated. For instance, the server could increase the price offered by a request to find it a match just before the deadline. The loan becomes a feedback to the reward system on the initiator of the task. After finalization, the agents proceed to establish connections for the requesters and the providers' resources at the local level. A proxy server of adjustable complexity could reside at the local resources to enable peer-to-peer transactions. The requests become jobs at the local resources and queue themselves according to the price offered and follow the local queuing discipline. This process does not require global coordination. The queuing status, including workload, will become feedback to update the local resource's agents at the blackboard. The global server contains a Metadatabase about tasks characteristics and enterprise requirements to support the blackboard. The server also includes an Agent-Base to create and manage the task agents online, which could number in the millions, according to users' instructions.

An alternative to going through the Blackboard is for a participant to initiate directly task agents that visit other task agents at other local sites to find-negotiate the matches and conduct auction when necessary, on their own within the virtual "match circle." This alternative is available to local sites that have sufficient computing power. In this case, the initiating participants will control the virtual auctions that their task agents started first (distributed computing); and hence simplify the computing load at the global server.

4. THE ENTERPRISE RESOURCES MARKET METHODS

The above architecture entails several major elements. Some of the key methods and techniques are adopted from our past research (Bouziane 1991; Cheung 1991; Hsu, Bouziane et al. 1991; Babin 1993). We adapt these results for the Enterprise Resources Market, and further develop them and the new elements not available currently to satisfy the requirements of the system. We discuss the details below.

4.1 The Agent Model: Task Agent, Agent-Base, and Metadatabase

Resource providers and users initiate their offers and requests through custom created task agents. They log on (remotely) to the Agent-Base at the exchange site and instruct it to create a task agent for their offers or requests. The software agents are uploaded to the local sites of the participants. They use the same mechanism to update or delete their agents. The participants can now initiate a task by launching the agent created to the Blackboard of the exchange site. The agent publishes its information content (see below) at the Blackboard, with possible subsequent modifications. The Blackboard uses this information to conduct matching, negotiation-auction, and assignment, as described in the next section on Blackboard.

The agent has three basic elements: the communicator, the information content, and the rule-base. The communicator includes header (e.g., ID or IP address, XML-SQL or inter-operation protocols, and other metadata and routines required for agent processing). We will consider the best practices in the field as well as the operating policies of the enterprise to determine the actual design of the communicator. The information content describes the conditions and semantics of the task according to certain representation methods acceptable to the enterprise. In any design, the conditions specify the price demanded or offered, the deadline, and processing requirements; while the semantics use either the common schema of the organization or, if one does not exist, the common dictionary of keywords to communicate to other agents the information nature of the task. The processing requirements include the type of resource offered or requested, job constraints and task status if the task belongs to an automated workflow (series of single tasks) or complex task. A complex task will be processed as a sequence of single tasks according to processing or workflow rules. The rule-base contains operating knowledge for conducting automatic negotiation, auction, and other similar behaviors, such as choices of pre-determined negotiation schemes. It also contains workflow rules and other logic for the processing of complex tasks. All agents follow a unified protocol regulated by the Agent-Base using the knowledge stored in the Metadatabase.

The Metadatabase contains a version of the communal or extended organization-wide common schema, or a common dictionary of keywords that the participants use, for information enterprise resources allocation. It, along with the proxy server (see Section 4.3), constitutes the connector of the artificial market through which the system plugs into the overall enterprise environment. While the proxy server provides physical connection in an API manner, the Metadatabase offers logical integration with the enterprise. If these common schema or keywords do not currently exist, then we need to develop the keywords with enterprise experts as an implementation effort. Alternatively, when the enterprise chooses to develop its own common schema from scratch, we could employ the Metadatabase model developed at Rensselaer over the past decade (Hsu, Bouziane et al. 1991; Babin and Hsu 1996; Cheung and Hsu 1996; Hsu 1996; Hsu and Pant 2000) to accomplish this purpose. The Metadatabase model employs a particular representation method based on the TSER information model to integrate enterprise information models, contextual knowledge, software resources (for inter-operation), and user-application families. These enterprise metadata are structured into a database on its own so that the community can query, manage, and evolve enterprise metadata resources through the Metadatabase for their tasks in the same manner as they could for regular data resources with a regular database. Therefore, the Metadatabase can be a repository of enterprise policies pertaining to the artificial market (such as rules about particular user-application families, entities, and relationships). Moreover, the scope of the representation method covers all three elements of the software agents; thus, the Metadatabase can also be a depot of re-usable objects or common raw materials (communication software, information content, and rules) from which the Agent-Base builds task agents. In any case, the provision or the construction of the common schema and/or keywords, regardless of the methods taken, would have to come from the enterprise experts in the extended organization. Without them, the proposed research would only simulate one for the final prototype.

One aspect of the Agent-Base is a method to mass-customize large amount of agents at run time. When the potential task agents at any one time could number thousands or even millions, and most of them are custom build, then we need an efficient way to create and manage these agents online and on the fly. We will use the Metadatabase to provide community resources required by mass production, and use the Agent-Base to customize the configuration of these resources for particular tasks. It will also support the owners of the agents to add ad-hoc information (e.g., specific data values of some entities, relationships, or attributes, and operating rules) and route them to the Metadatabase for possible inclusion into its content. Another aspect is the ability to automatically update the metadata contents of agents when these metadata are changed at the Metadatabase. This capability, unique to the Agent-Base model, is very useful for maintaining the logical consistency across agents, or the integrity of the agent community. The third aspect is a log of the task agents currently active at the Blackboard. This design allows the software agent to be a persistent surrogate (24/7) at the market for conducting asynchronous negotiation, among other things, to enhance reliability and performance. Thus, the Agent-Base is both a management shell and a gathering of active agents.

We need to fine-tune the agent design, the Metadatabase model, and the Agent-Base of the Enterprise Resources Market for particular enterprises. However, the general designs available now provide a good starting point for the particularization effort. Both the Metadatabase and the Agent-Base could be implemented on a commercial, stand-alone database management system such as Oracle. We envision the necessary user interfaces of these components to be added shells of the database using its built-in facilities.

4.2   The Blackboard: Match, Negotiation-Auction, and Assignment

The Blackboard is the regular, default mechanism for the Enterprise Resources Market to serve the agents and conduct match, negotiation-auction, and assignment. This engine maintains a list of all tasks published by agents, including their information contents, conduct matching and negotiation, and finalize the assignment. It also consults with the Metadatabase for the latest enterprise policies to avoid chaos at the artificial market; one of these responsibilities is to break ties and ascertain that all (worthy) tasks find a match before their deadlines.

The basic logic of match goes this way. For a given task, it first satisfies the semantic constraints by looking for counterparts possessing the same information content. The match is based on metadata, either from common schema or keywords, and can either be exact or partial. The software agent specifies the rules. The Blackboard could either incorporates the rules in its matching (custom match) or inform the logged agent of the result of standard match for it to exercise the rules. When semantic constraints are met, the matching proceeds to conditions including price, deadline, and other requirements. If single perfect match exists, then the Blackboard will assign the task to the resources matched. If multiple perfect matches are found, then a round of auction amongst them will decide the final assignment. If only partial matches are found, then the task enters negotiation. The negotiation could be automated where the logged agents concerned use their rules to find an optimal match and break ties by auction; or, the agents could inform the task initiators and have a round of modification of the original conditions – i.e., human intervened negotiation. On the other hand, if no match, perfect or partial, is found, then the agent and/or the initiator could update the task information content depending on whether the difficulty is caused by semantics or by conditions. The Blackboard will post current market conditions – e.g., statistics of bids, usage patterns of keywords, and status of hot issues – to facilitate the modification and negotiation. The initiators could also proactively update the task agents stored at the local site and re-launch it to replace the old one. Certain conditions, especially those related to workload at local resources, would be suitable for automatic update from the participant sites. The Blackboard intervenes only on an as-needed, exceptional basis to break ties and enforce enterprise policies. For example, it could check on certain types of requesting tasks that have no match and increase their offering prices on a loan basis to find them a match on or near the deadline.

The assignment phase is essentially a notification of the connections that the tasks should establish with their resources. It entails an update of the communicator of the logged task agent by the Agent-Base, if necessary, to prepare it to communicate with the proxy server at the destination resources site. The update agent will then upload to the task initiating site and initiate a peer-to-peer transaction from there. Now, the task agent is ready to subscribe to the resources; namely, connect to their system.

It is well known that the computational complexity of traditional scheduling algorithms (global control) is NP-hard; while the complexity of sorting (according to price) is linear, $O(N)$ with N being the number of tasks. Thus, the self-scheduling nature of the Enterprise Resources Market assures a very efficient regime of computation with complexity in linear to low order of polynomial (including negotiation and feedback). Therefore, the artificial market is scalable exponentially in theory; i.e., its computational efficiency allows it to expand virtually freely. However, this is not the case with most other schedulers, whose scalability is inherently limited by its computational complexity.

4.3 The Proxy Server: Peer-to-Peer Transaction and Systems Inter-operation

The proxy server is a software system that the artificial market adds to local resources sites and resides there. It accomplishes two basic jobs towards enabling the computing connection of the exchange side with the participant side: systems inter-operation and peer-to-peer transaction. The server interacts with the exchange site and collaborates with the Agent-Base to store, maintain, and process (launch) the software agents owned by its local site, as well as to respond (execute) to the call of task agents from other sites. In this capacity, it functions as the server of the local site for all task agents initiated at the site but processed elsewhere at the Blackboard or other local sites. Thus, it executes the workflow logic for its complex tasks to, e.g., sequentially launch the component single tasks and maintain the overall task status. The server offers a data standard for the task agents to communicate between themselves. The exact design will depend on the enterprise requirements; but a good, standing design is to use XML-SQL. That is, the proxy server will have a standard protocol to receive and process task agents for information transfer. Part of the protocol is a standard schema for view tables that the proxy server maintains for the local databases to use. It works two ways. First, the local database publishes the select content that it slates to share with the artificial market at the proxy server, using the format provided by the latter. The information requesting task agents can then query the view tables to retrieve or transfer the selected content. Second, if its own task agents transfer in content from other resources, then the input is stored as view tables for the database to acquire under its own management. The queue discipline at the proxy server is self-scheduling based on prices. However, if the requesting task from outside is to use the computing facility for data processing, as opposed to information retrieval, then the proxy server passes it as a regular job to the local system and follow the local queue discipline. In a similar way, it monitors the work load, task status, and other relevant data of the host server to update its task agents at the Agent-Base and elsewhere in the system.

The proxy server also controls peer-to-peer negotiation, including matching and auction, as described in the next sub-section, if the local site has sufficient computing power to invoke this option. In this capacity, the proxy server launches its task agents to visit task agents publishing on proxy servers at other local sites, as well as prepare them for negotiation with visiting agents from other participants. The proxy server from which the task agent first (time stamp) initiates a peer-to-peer negotiation in the community will function as a mini-Blackboard during the life of the negotiation. The basic logic of the Blackboard applies here, except that the initiating task agents call on other sites rather than other agents posting onto its proxy server. As such, a proxy server might control several concurrent auctions involving different tasks at different sites, and the community might have numerous such auctions controlled by different proxy servers at numerous local sites at the same time; all are autonomous to the global server. In this mode, a proxy server will maintain a list of visiting task agents and matches its own task agents against them at the time the participant publishes them.

The employment of proxy servers allows for peer-to-peer transaction and hence concludes the assurance of the computational efficiency promised by the price-based Blackboard. Peer-to-peer transaction is advantageous to the environment for these basic reasons: (1) it allows for the participants' direct control of all tasks originating at their site as well as tasks being processed there, and hence simplifies the global control requirements and work load; (2) it supports distributed updates and processing of agents based on local conditions; and (3) it provides a backup to the Blackboard. Furthermore, it also contributes an open and scalable way to connect any number of local databases and other resources into the Enterprise Resources Market without interrupting the operation of the market. Along with the Metadatabase, which offers an open and scalable way to incorporate any number of information models into the market on the fly, and the Blackboard, which promises computational scalability, these three elements of the Enterprise Resources Market make this design uniquely open and scalable.

An implementation of the model can adopt the best practices in the field to build the proxy server for the enterprise, in light of the new agent model and the Blackboard. A reference point for the technology is the commonly available products such as Apache server, which is extendable with JAVA-J2EE, PERL, and other general purpose programming languages. Although one needs to design it, the proxy server has many mature technologies to choose from for its implementation.

4.4   Peer-to-Peer Negotiation: Virtual and Distributed Mini-Blackboards

Peer-to-peer computing has a general complexity of $O(N^2)$ which hinders scaling-up. We develop a new basic logical structure, the match circles, to denote the group of nodes (local sites) whose tasks match. Pair-wise computing is unnecessary within a match circle once it is recognized. Thus, a circle will have a node serving as its mini-Blackboard and thereby reduce the computing complexity. Since a local site can have a number of simultaneous tasks alive in the community, it can belong to a number of simultaneous match circles. Thus, both the circles and the mini-Blackboard are virtual and task-based. This way, the overall complexity of the peer-to-peer computing is primarily the number of such virtual circles, which is arguably much less than the theoretical upper bound. We elaborate on this idea below.

The Agent-Base maintains a global protocol for determining timestamps for all task agents initiating a negotiation, which starts with a search for matches at other local sites and finishes when an assignment is finalized after, if necessary, auctioning among multiple matches. The negotiation at the matching phase is concerned with task constraints, while it is about the objective function when auctioning. The initiating task agent, the one with the earliest timestamp among all agents that matched, has the control of the negotiation. Its proxy server first launches a round of search where the task agent looks for matches at (all) other local sites in the community in a purely peer-to-peer manner. If a single perfect match is found within a pre-determined time period, then the proxy server acts according to the nature of the task: for requesting task, it obtains necessary inter-operation parameters or routines from the Agent-Base for the task agent and sends it to queue at the matching site through the proxy server at that site; and for offering task, it informs the proxy server of the match task to launch the requesting agent. Optionally, the proxy server could also contain a reduced copy of the Metadatabase to allow it augmenting its task agents with the inter-operation data. If multiple matches exist, then the proxy server conducts an auctioning session where it sends out asking prices, iteratively, to the matches in the manner of traditional auctions – i.e., the proxy server singly controls the auction session. The result will either be a single meeting of the best price – in which case the proxy server assigns the task as mentioned above, or a declaration of failure of the auction which results in a deletion of the current task. The participant in the latter case can opt to re-initiate the task or re-create a new task agent.

If no perfect match is found when the time expires, then the initiating task agent everywhere starts a round of lock-step, pair-wise negotiation with its host agents. Each pair of negotiation is independent of all other pairs under the initiating task agent's autonomous control, which uses the same negotiating regime to proceed. The regime could be rule-based, staged modules, or any appropriate design, as long as it uses definitive steps to define and control its gives and takes, with each step associated with a certain time window. Thus, all pair-wise, simultaneous negotiations at all local sites are at the same steps at all times. Each step modifies certain constraints in certain manner within each window, and the proxy server terminates the negotiation at the first moment when a perfect match or matches are found. At the conclusion of each step of the negotiation for matches (on constraints), the task agent returns the matches (when achieved) with an indicator of the step during which they are obtained, along with the identification of the local proxy servers of the matched task agents. The initiating proxy server could use the indicator to determine the matches in the assumption that modifications are reversely favorable in the sequence of steps and hence the earlier the matches the more preferable. Thus, if some negotiations are lagging behind because of their local queuing situations or any other reasons, then they could preempt incumbent results (including auctions) when they report matches back to the initiating proxy server. However, the proxy server could also opt to ignore late results whenever the auction is underway. The task agents use the time-based progression of negotiation to synchronize virtually their autonomous processing. The initiating proxy server, i.e., the mini-Blackboard in this case for the round of negotiation, does not actively control the processing of its task agent at each local site, but only determine the matches from all reported results. When the time expires without any matches found, the task agent ceases to exist and the participant could either revive it or forgo it. The peer-to-peer design allows a proxy server to control the negotiations (matching and auctioning) of its task agents, individually as well as collectively (to manage its own local resources), and thereby promote distributed computing. There could be many proxy servers controlling many concurrent negotiation sessions in the community at any time, each of which is a virtual mini-Blackboard for the match circle, or the virtual group of matched task agents.

4.5   Implementation Model: Organizational Metrics and Data Standard

To implement the artificial market in the enterprise environment, we need to investigate some of the organizational issues, especially how to map the pricing model to organizational control metrics and how to inter-operate the Enterprise Resources Market with other functions and systems. We assume that the extended organization uses a budget model to control the overall allocation of resources to operating units and individuals. The model will create artificial funds (either of money or of fungible credit) for participants of Enterprise Resources Market, and periodically deposit or adjust them according to their overall performance at the market over the period, among other things, on an off-line basis. In addition, the market maintains these funds and will automatically adjust them for the participants after each transaction to reflect their revenues (sales) or payments (purchases) in a manner similar to a bank. Thus, individuals and operating units do not exchange money directly, but their purchasing power as recognized by the market. The bids, therefore, reflect the perceived value of the resources requested or offered by the participants. To make the scheme work, the fund owners must have control of their funds and the ability to use surplus for real world purposes such as hiring people or purchasing facilities. Thus, the market itself is the first mechanism to measure performance, reward the participants, and thereby reallocate resources. The managers of the participants will also assess the performance of resources in terms of value added to their missions; that is, the quality and quantity of information provided and utilized. They could measure the value in terms of how many people have used and benefited from the offerings (sales) and how actively people seek out for useful information. The system will generate market statistics on problems (e.g., loans), requests, offerings, transactions, connections, keyword usage (hot topics), as well as accounting and scheduling logs. Results are performance feedback to the managers for the budgeting process and reward systems. This periodic review assisted by market statistics is the second line of control and reward for resource allocation.

We need to study the optimal way to design the pricing model for an implementation so as to best fit the organizational metrics of performance evaluation and reward. Furthermore, for organizational evaluation, the implementation also should consider developing the possibilities of collaboration with other enterprise management functions. For instance, the patterns of subscription (connection) reveal the need for new or ad-hoc channels of communication or workflow processes. Thus, these data could feed into such models as organizational networks and processes.

The data standard issue concerns inter-operating local databases within the domain of the enterprise and possible collaboration with other enterprise functions. The first aspect is a matter of information integration and data interchange protocols. As discussed above in the sections on the agent model and the proxy server, we propose to use the current organizational specification of keywords or common schema to represent data semantics and store them into the Metadatabase, to achieve logical information integration; and use the proxy server to handle data interchange. This approach is well established in industry; in addition, the above sections also offered realistic alternatives for the development of Market data standard. We are confident that in the case of actual implementation, one can adopt the best practices in the field of e-business and database integration to recommend a data standard for the enterprise and make the artificial market work as designed. At present, we propose common technologies including XML-SQL, relational databases, and Internet-based computing protocols. The data format required for collaboration with other enterprise systems will come from these sources. We will continue to investigate these issues and hopefully recommend some general designs as the field matures.

4.6   Open Common Schema: a Metadatabase for Extensible Information Integration

The section on the Agent Model provides a Metadatabase to represent data semantics of all resources in the enterprise. This task usually corresponds to developing a common schema at the high end of integration effort, or a reference dictionary of keywords at the low end. Current practices in the field at both ends have certain drawbacks: available common schema methods tend to be hard to develop and too rigid to maintain, while keywords might not cover the full semantics contained in information models (especially relationships and contextual knowledge - processes). An alternative is to base the common schema on an ontology (the basic structure of semantics at a meta-level), rather than on tenuous instances of practice. The Metadatabase model is such a design, offering an open, scalable and integrated repository of enterprise information models (in the form of metadata), constructed on a minimal ontology of generic information modeling concepts per se. The ontology is comparable in concept to the Information Resources Dictionary System (IRDS) effort of NIST (see (Hsu 1996)) and similar approaches in the current Enterprise Integration community. However, it differs fundamentally from designs that generalize application logic for an entire domain. The methodology-based ontology offers efficiency and simplicity (minimalism), but is limited to the applicability of the method on which the design is based. For the Metadatabase, the basis is the Two-Stage Entity-Relationship model, an extended entity-relationship-attribute model. Previous works have shown the model to be scalable (i.e., metadata independence) (Hsu 1996) and capable of incorporating rules (Hsu, Tao et al. 1993) and supporting global query processing across multiple databases (Cheung and Hsu 1996).

The icons of the Metadatabase structure, or the graphical representation of the ontology, shown in Fig. 2-4, represent either a table of metadata or a particular type of integrity control rules. The ontology in Fig. 2-4 extends slightly the previous Metadatabase structure by also including user words and cases (as in case-based reasoning), to enhance the extension of the model. The metadata include subjects and views, entity-relationship models, contextual knowledge in the form of rules, application and user definitions, database definitions and database objects. User-words are defined as ordered pairs (class, object). Classes include Applications, Subjects, EntRels (entity-relationship), Items, Values, and Operators; all of which are metadata tables as shown in Fig. 2-4. Objects are instances (contents) of these classes. An object is uniquely identified by an ordered quadruple (Item name, EntRel name, Subject name, Application name) as well as an identifier. A case consists of a problem definition and a solution, but not the usual outcome, because the Metadatabase contains the complete domain knowledge needed. New problems (e.g., exceptions to general policies) would use the problem definition to find the (best) matching cases and apply the associated solutions to them. A set of metadata for a task describes the problem definition, and its interpretation defines the solution. Cases strengthen the Blackboard's ability to perform real time matching and assignment of tasks when uncertainty arises. As such, the Metadatabase collects local information models as the elements (metadata entries) constituting the common schema.

The common schema so constructed, as a Metadatabase, will be able to accommodate changes, including deletion, addition, and modification of information models for local resources. For instance, when a new local resource is added to the Market, the necessary "registration" effort will be to create an information model using the TSER methodology for the new resource (either by the local participants or by the Market experts), and add the information model as new metadata entries to the appropriate meta-tables of the Metadatabase (e.g., SQL Insert statements). This process is amenable to automation using a CASE tool. The Metadatabase does not need to shut down at any time during the update, since the operation is really a regular database job. After this logical connection, the Market will install a proxy server fine-tuned for the new resource in the local environment, as described before. This installment does not interfere with the regular operation of the (rest of the) Market, and hence the whole addition process will not affect any existing local systems nor the on-going tasks at the Market. Once the process is completed, the new resource takes part immediately and automatically in the Market. Other changes are similarly self-contained and autonomous. Therefore, the design offers an open common schema to enable extensible information integration for the community and thereby facilitate it to become open and scalable, as well.

The Metadatabase has been tested extensively in LAN, WAN, and even Internet-based environments at some industrial companies. However, it has not been deployed for an open community such as the extended information enterprises targeted here. Thus, its development into the common schema will represent a new contribution to the filed.

In a broad sense, the proposed technology contributes intellectually to two hard problems: real time global resource allocation and information integration for extended enterprises; both of which are critical to IT-based organizations. Its extensions on the previous scheduling regimes include its true, price-driven market mechanism to provide comprehensive performance evaluation, feedback, and resources reallocation. This new mechanism is made possible by its new agent model and the extensions to previous exchange technology. The industrial exchange model has always called for the use of agent technology, but actual practices tend to stop short because of insufficient capacity for large-scale agents management. This research fills in the gap with the new Agent-Base using the proven Metadatabase technology. It further extends the previous results to allow for peer-to-peer negotiation and information sharing, where traditional exchanges tend to limit the data transactions to the processing of business documents and straightforward transfer of files. When we can show to have achieved the intended results, we will have accomplished a good progress toward resolving these two problems.

Furthermore, the new results amount to a general agent-based, peer-to-peer, publish and subscribe model applicable to a class of problems in the digital society. Examples encompass naturally the management of global (virtual) enterprises; but they also extend to such novel areas as community collaboration in for-profit or non-profit settings. A particular vision would be for persons, companies, and organizations to buy and sell information resources from the universal Internet community on a task-by-task basis. As the concept of an exchange is general and far reaching, so does the notion of the new model. The new results make it feasible technically to realize some of the new visions of exchange in practice.

Chapter 4

THE CORE LOGIC OF THE TWO-STAGE COLLABORATION MODEL
Information Matching

1. OVERVIEW

The Two-Stage Collaboration Model (TSCM) engenders a new global query method that supports self-determination of independent databases. The TSCM accomplishes this primarily through the introduction of *information matching*, which enables the new two-sided collaboration regime (see Chapter 1, Section 2), and the *export databases* that serve as a proxy (image) in the TSCM for private and protected enterprise databases. The export database is also supported by the new global query paradigm, where a participant specifies the particular data resources that are to be shared from the enterprise database, but which are actually stored and offered from the export database during regular operation of the TSCM. Multiple such images in different representations can be supported simultaneously in the new paradigm.

The new, defining fundamental results developed in this research are concerned with information matching; so we discuss these results herein before we present the architectural design of the TSCM. As mentioned above, export databases submit subscription queries and/or publishing queries. They are matched in the first stage to determine the global database queries to be executed in the second stage. The matching process requires a number of steps to determine, to what extent and of what type matches exist, if any. A match can come from a single publishing export database or a joining of multiple export databases, for example.

The first step of matching is to identify the sets of publishing queries that contain all the required data items. They are qualified as **item feasible**, as each set may be used to extract all the data items required. Second, we verify that all export databases in an item feasible set (if containing more than one) can indeed join to produce meaningful information. This is done by verifying the existence of common data items among publishing queries within the set. Such sets are said to be **join feasible**, as we may identify join conditions between the different queries within the set. This verification process may result in the addition of new publishing queries to the set to make the (extended) set join feasible. Third, we verify that the constraints on a join feasible set match the constraints on the subscription query. When this is the case, the set is said to be **constraint feasible**. Finally, the best constraint feasible set is selected for allocation.

2.   THE NEW ELEMENTS OF GLOBAL QUERY

It is necessary, for the purposes of this research, to rethink the concept of a global query to achieve the benefits described above. A global query is therefore represented in this new context as a subscription query (or information request). This new connotation emphasizes that a global query no longer exists as a single execution or process, but now that it can exist for an extended period of time, "connected" to its target database. Similarly, publication queries can exist for an extended duration, but add the facility to declare what content should be shared from an enterprise database. The overall concept of global query in general is also modified; in the TSCM context it is considered as a two-stage process. In the first stage, subscription queries are matched with publication queries to associate information seekers with information providers. In the second phase, match information obtained from the first stage are used to obtain results from the corresponding information provider(s) using traditional query processing methods. To establish these new concepts, a technical analysis is employed to formally characterize the subscription and publication queries, below.

Let Q^S: a set containing search terms, where a search term is a data item $i \in I$ and $Q^S \subseteq \bigcup_{k=1}^{n} M_k$

Let Q^P: a set containing search terms, where a search term is a data item $i \in I$ and $Q^P \subseteq M_k$

Let I: the set of all data items, where $I \subseteq M_k$

Let M_k: the metadata from a single system, which includes structural and functional information, and $\bigcup_{k=1}^{n} M_k$ the collective set of metadata from all systems, made available by the Metadatabase.

Let R: a set containing rules associated with a query, where each contains a set of conditions C, and optionally a set of actions A.

Let C: a set of conditions used to qualify the search terms in the query, or the query in general. There are three classes: *selection conditions* (C^S), *join conditions* (C^J) and *negotiation conditions* (C^N).

Given these definitions a subscription query takes the following form:

$$(Q^S, R \mid Q^S \subseteq \bigcup_{k=1}^{n} M_k \wedge R = (C, A)), \text{ where } C \subseteq C^S \cup C^J \cup C^N \qquad (1)$$

To clarify, a subscription query is defined as a set containing search terms indicated as data items, and a set of rules, where the data items are limited to the boundaries of the global information model, and the rules (which qualify or constrain the data items, and the query in general) represent a combination of selection, join and negotiation conditions, and actions. It is necessary to emphasize that the subscription query can be constructed from any element, i.e. data items, in the entire global data model.

This is not the case however for a publication query, which derives its search terms from an individual system. A publication query can only be provided by the owner of a system, and so the contents of the query are derived from the sub-schema of the global data model that represents this particular system. Accordingly, a publication query takes the following form:

$$(Q^P, R \mid Q^P \subseteq M_k \wedge R = (C, A)), \text{ where } C \subseteq C^S \cup C^J \cup C^N \qquad (2)$$

It must be emphasized here that the content of a publication query is restricted to the sub-schema of the Metadatabase, M_k that corresponds to the enterprise database. The scope of data items available to a query therefore represents the fundamental difference between a publication query and a subscription query. These definitions present the opportunity to formalize the entire lifecycle of this new global query method. This begins with the next section.

3.   QUERY MATCHING: IDENTIFYING COMPLEMENTARY QUERIES

The first stage in the TSCM is concerned with the matching of queries, which means identifying queries that are the complement of a supplied query. These complementary queries contain matching search terms and conditions. This matching stage is concluded with the allocation of a query, which identifies the best match among those found earlier, if multiple matches are found. Otherwise, the allocation of the match is trivial. The second stage in the TSCM is concerned with the execution of the query, which submits the allocated query to the corresponding export database for execution. The basic logic of matching involves three steps, as follows.

3.1   Step 1 – Identify Matching Data Items

The query matching process is defined as follows: Given a query S, identify a complementary query $q \in Q$, such that $q \cap S \neq \varnothing$. Essentially, matching queries must contain common data items. The query S can be considered as a subscription query or publication query, and similarly a query $q \in Q$, identified from a set of Q, can be considered a publication query or subscription query. The match process always finds the complement of the supplied query. As demonstrated in Fig. 4-1, the match process given queries $q \in Q$ and S produces four classes of results: (a) an *exact* match, (b) a *superset* match, (c) a *subset* match, and (d) an *intersect* match.

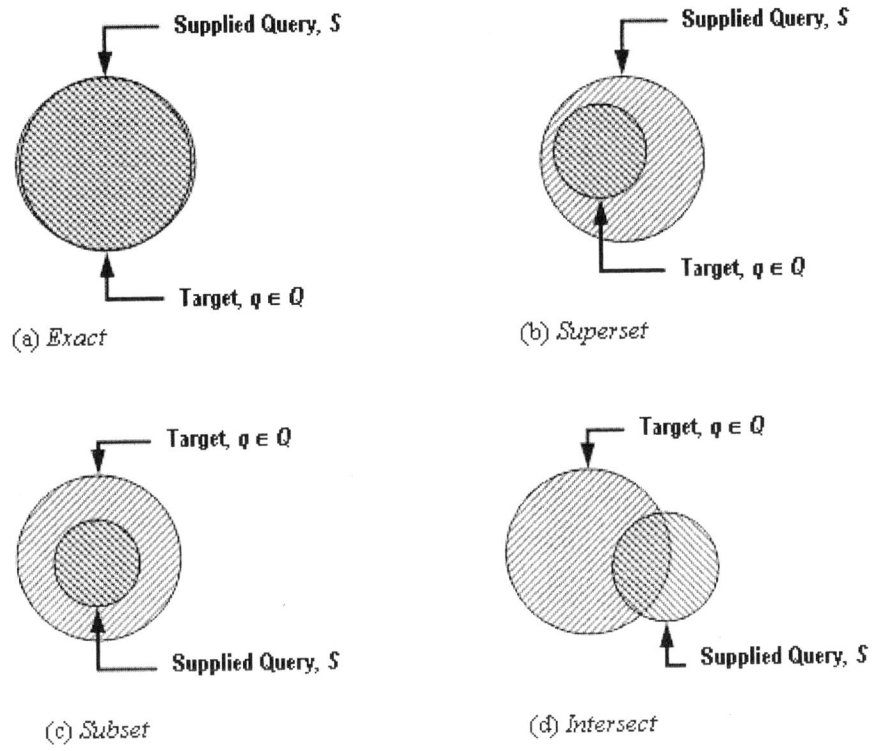

Figure 4-1. Match Classes Determined from Algorithm 1

Definition: An exact match indicates that the data items in $q \in Q$ are equivalent to those in S, i.e. the complementary queries have the same number of data items, which share the same semantics, and syntax. This is formally established in the following statement:

Exact: *Card* $(S) = Card (q \cap S)$ and *Card* $(q \cap S) = Card (q)$, where *Card* $(q \cap S) > 0$.

Definition: A superset match indicates that the number of items matched is less than that specified in S but equivalent to those defined in a $q \in Q$. This is established as,

Superset: *Card* $(S) > Card (q \cap S)$ and *Card* $(q \cap S) = Card (q)$ where *Card* $(q \cap S) > 0$.

Definition: A subset match indicates that the number of items matched is equivalent to the number of items in S, but less than the number of items that exist in $q \in Q$. This is established as,

Subset: *Card* (S) = *Card* $(q \cap S)$ and *Card* $(q \cap S)$ < *Card* (q) where $q \in Q$.

Definition: An intersect match demonstrates that the queries contain common items. That is the number of items matched is less than the number of items that exist in both S and $q \in Q$. That is,

Intersect: *Card* (S) > *Card* $(q \cap S)$ and *Card* $(q \cap S)$ < *Card* (q), where $q \in Q$.

The algorithm illustrated in Table 4-1 summarizes the match of S and $q \in Q$. For each $q \in Q$, if the match engine determines that S and $q \in Q$ contain common items, it will count these data items and classify the match according to the aforementioned definitions. It returns the set of queries that match the supplied query S.

Table 4-1. **Algorithm 1**: *Matching* (S)

Let I: the set of all search terms (data items)
Let S: the *query*, containing items, $i \in I$, and $S \subseteq I$
Let Q: the set of all queries, each containing items $i \in I$ and $Q \subseteq I$
Let Q': the set of all queries that match S, such that $\exists i \in S$
Let *Select* (S): the set of queries that match S.
Let *Type* (S): the type of query, which belongs to one of two query classes *request* or *offer*.
Let R: the set of queries Q that match S qualified by the class of match *Exact* (R^E), *Superset* (R^P), *Subset* (R^B), and *Intersect* (R^I).

$Q' \leftarrow$ *Select* $(q \mid q \in Q \wedge q \cap S \neq \varnothing \wedge q \notin$ *Type* $(S))$
For each $q \in Q'$
   If *Card* (S) = *Card* $(q \cap S)$ and *Card* $(q \cap S)$ = *Card* (q)
     $R^E \leftarrow R^E \cup q$
   Else-If *Card* (S) > *Card* $(q \cap S)$ and *Card* $(q \cap S)$ = *Card* (q)
     $R^P \leftarrow R^P \cup q$
   Else-If *Card* (S) = *Card* $(q \cap S)$ and *Card* $(q \cap S)$ < *Card* (q)
     $R^B \leftarrow R^B \cup q$
   Else-If *Card* (S) > *Card* $(q \cap S)$ and *Card* $(q \cap S)$ < *Card* (q)
     $R^I \leftarrow R^I \cup q$
   End-If
End-For
Return R

3.2 Step 2 – Combine Queries to Identify a Feasible Solution

If a query $q \in Q$ that contain all the data items in the supplied query cannot be identified, that is, if an exact or subset match (recall, this is from the perspective of *S*) has not be found, but a superset and intersect match (See Fig. 4-2) has been found, then an advanced round of matching is entered into to attempt to find a solution for *S*. Here, the results from Step 1 (See Section 3.1) are combined (that is, superset and intersect) and each combination is evaluated to determine if it contains the data items found in the supplied query, *S*. The resulting combination queries are classified as, (1) *combination exact* match, (2) *combination superset* match, (2) *combination subset* match, and (4) *combination intersect* match, where each, respectively, is the analogue of the classification defined in Section 3.1 and in Table 4-1 above.

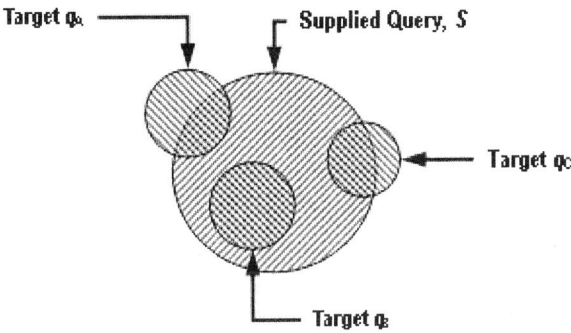

Figure 4-2. Conditions Required for a Combination Match

3.3   Item and Join Feasible Solutions

A combination exact or combination subset match does not indicate that a solution for the query *S* has been found; rather, only that the disparate queries combined, contain data items common to *S*. This is considered an *item feasible* solution. To be otherwise considered a *join feasible* solution, the queries $q \in Q$ that constitute the combination query must be logically connected. This is illustrated with the following example:

Table 4-2. Combination Match Example

$S = \{item_1, item_2, item_3, item_4\}$
$q_A = \{item_1, item_2, item_n, item_{n+1}\}$
$q_B = \{item_2, item_3\}$
$q_C = \{item_4, item_m, item_{m+1}\}$

Let S, q_A, q_B, and q_C correspond to the subscription query and publication queries respectively that are illustrated in Fig. 4-2 and Table 4-2 above. As indicated in the illustrations, q_A, q_B, and q_C match S on particular data items, and each with the class of match specified in Fig. 4-2 above. For example, q_A matches S on data items, $item_1$ and $item_2$. The union of q_A, q_B, and q_C, which is denoted as q_{ABC} is the combination query that contains all data items found in S; however this is only regarded as an *item feasible* solution, if the intersection of q_A, q_B, and q_C is empty. If q_{ABC} is to be the more valuable and meaningful *join feasible* solution for S then there must be logical relationships among q_A, q_B, and q_C, or the intersection of q_A, q_B, and q_C is not empty. In the event that q_A, q_B, and q_C is empty, the Metadatabase is employed to evaluate these *item feasible* solutions, whereas logical connection between queries are determined from the global data model.

In this specific example, the intersection of q_A and q_B is item feasible and join feasible, since the union contain common items in S, and the intersection of q_A and q_B is not empty.

To extend this example, find that the union q_{ABC} also contains data items common to S, but there is no apparent connection between q_A, q_B and q_C. In this case the Metadatabase may be consulted for information, which would need to determine that that the q_C is dependent on attributes in q_A or q_B for this to be considered a join feasible solution. Otherwise, it would not be possible determine the join feasibility of q_{ABC}. The following definitions summarize these findings:

Let S: a query used as the input in our match algorithm

Let Q: a set of queries that the query S will be matched against

Let IF: the set of item feasible solutions

Let JF: the set of join feasible solutions

Let JF': the set of join feasible solutions resulting from a combination query

Let R^E, R^P, R^B, R^I: be defined as shown in Table 4-1.

Definition 1:

$$\forall q \in R^E \cup R^B \Rightarrow q \in IF \text{ and } q \in JF$$

For each query q, where S is an exact and/or subset q, then the query q by default is item feasible and join feasible.

Definition 2:

$$JF = R^E \cup R^B \cup JF' \text{ where } JF' = \left(\bigcup_i q_i\right) \in IF \Leftrightarrow \left(\bigcup_i q_i\right) \cap S = S$$

A query is join feasible if it satisfies *Definition 1*, and if it is a component of a combination query $\left(\bigcup_i q_i\right)$, where $\left(\bigcup_i q_i\right)$ is item feasible and contains all the data items in S.

Definition 3:

$$\left(\bigcup_i q_i\right) \in JF' \Rightarrow \forall q \in R^P \cup R^I \mid \forall q \in IF, \exists q' \in IF \neq \varnothing \mid q \cap q' \neq \varnothing$$

A combination query $\left(\bigcup_i q_i\right)$ is join feasible if the queries in the combination belong to the set where S is a superset of, or intersects q, and if the queries q_i in $\left(\bigcup_i q_i\right)$ intersect and contain common data items.

Algorithm 2 in Table 4-3 determines if a combination query is feasible. The feasible combination query (or queries) that result contains the greatest number of data items common to S.

Let S: the set of search terms defined in a query, where search term is a data item $i \in I$

Let R: the set of queries that match S derived from Algorithm 1 and qualified by the class of match *Exact, Superset, Subset,* and *Intersect*

Let R': the set of queries that match S derived from R and qualified by the class of match *Superset* and *Intersect*

Let M: the set of messages sent among the nodes (queries) R' in the current cycle

Let N: the set of pending messages to be sent among the nodes R' in the next cycle

Let P: the set of enumerated combinations of R'

Let P_{best}: The current best solution for the algorithm.

Let p_{best}: The value (cardinality) of the current best solution

Let $p_{include}$: The set of data items that must be included to create a join feasible solution using the Shortest Path Algorithm.

Let Initialize (B): returns a set of messages containing an identifier for the source of the message, and the data items contained in the set B.

Let n: The number of cycles for the algorithm to run.

Let ShortestPath (T): calls the shortest path algorithm for the given set of entity-relationships, T and returns the set of items required to logically connect T.

Let getEntRel (P): determines the entity-relationship(s) for the given combination P.

Let JoinFeasible(P): determine if the given combination query P is logically connected.

Table 4-3. **Algorithm 2**: Combination Matching (R)

$P_{best} \leftarrow \varnothing$
$P_{negotiate} \leftarrow \varnothing$
$R' \leftarrow R \mid R \notin R^E \wedge R \notin R^B$
$M \leftarrow Initialize\ (R')$
$N \leftarrow \varnothing$
$P \leftarrow \varnothing$
$n \leftarrow Card\ (R')$
$n_0 \leftarrow 1$
$p_{best} \leftarrow 0$
While $n_0 < n$
  For each $m \in M$
    For each $r \in R'$
      If $Card\ ((m \cup r) - m) > 0$ and $(m \cup r) \notin P$
        If $Card\ ((m \cup r) \cap S) > p_{best}$
          If $JoinFeasible\ (m \cup r)$
            $P_{best} \leftarrow P_{best} \cup (m \cup r)$
            $p_{best} = Card\ ((m \cup r) \cap S)$
          Else-If $ShortestPath\ (getEntRel\ (m \cup r)) \cup (m \cup r) - (m \cup r) \neq \varnothing$
            $P_{negotiate} \leftarrow P_{negotiate} \cup (m \cup r) \cup ShortestPath\ (getEntRel\ (m \cup r))$
          End-If
        Else-If $Card\ ((m \cup r) \cap S) = p_{best}$
          If $JoinFeasible\ (m \cup r)$
            $P_{best} \leftarrow P_{best} \cup (m \cup r)$
            $p_{best} = Card\ ((m \cup r) \cap S)$
          Else-If $ShortestPath\ (getEntRel\ (m \cup r)) \cup (m \cup r) - (m \cup r) \neq \varnothing$
            $P_{negotiate} \leftarrow P_{negotiate} \cup (m \cup r) \cup ShortestPath\ (getEntRel\ (m \cup r))$
          End-If
        End-If
        $P \leftarrow P \cup (m \cup r)$
        $N \leftarrow N \cup (m \cup r)$
      End-If
    End-For
  End-For
  $M \leftarrow N$
  $N \leftarrow \varnothing$
  $n_0 = n_0 + 1$
End-While
Return P_{best}

The primary function of Algorithm 2 is the one of message sending between nodes. Each query resulting from Algorithm 1 constitutes a node in Algorithm 2, and each node generates a unique message. Each message has an identifier that corresponds to the query name, and the attributes of the query constitutes the body of the message. At the start of the algorithm, the number of cycles the algorithm should run is determined, which corresponds to the number of queries found, *Count* ($R^P \cup R'$) in Algorithm 1, minus 1. Table 4-4 illustrates the combinations of three queries, q_A, q_B, and q_C, where $q_i \in R^P \cup R'$. Round 1 is ignored since this correspond directly with the elements of $R^P \cup R'$, and so rounds 2 and 3 identify the remaining nodes for processing.

Table 4-4. Evaluation of Combined Queries

Round	Combinations
1	q_A, q_B, q_C
2	q_{AB}, q_{AC}, q_{BC}
3	q_{ABC}

In the first cycle of the algorithm each node broadcasts its message, while the algorithm records all combined queries created as a result of the broadcast, and ignores duplicates that it may find. A broadcasted message received at a node has its message body combined with the contents of the node, and a combination query is created. The order in the combination is not significant; duplicate combination queries are created but are ignored by the algorithm as previously mentioned. If a combination query shares data items with the input query S, then the number of shared items constitutes p_{best}, if this number is greater than an earlier round of processing then we test the join feasibility of the query and return new solutions p_{best} and P_{best} if the function returns true. If a join feasible solution cannot be found then the modified *Shortest Path Algorithm* (See Appendix A-2 determines if the entities and relationships to which the data items in the queries belong, are logically connected (See Definition 4 below). The *getEntRel* function provides this aforementioned functionality. This process is repeated if p_{best} is unchanged in the current round of processing.

Definition 4:

$$ShortestPath\left(\bigcup_i q_i\right) \in JF' \Rightarrow \forall q \in R^P \cup R' \mid \forall q \in IF, \neg\exists\, q' \in IF \neq \varnothing \mid q \cap$$

$$q' = \varnothing \wedge ShortestPath\left(\bigcup_i q_i\right) \neq \varnothing$$

The *Shortest Path Algorithm* attempts to determine a join feasible solution from an item feasible combination query, where the set of queries that constitute the combination query are disjoint. The Shortest Path Algorithm therefore searches for additional metadata, which logically connects these disjoint queries, perhaps allowing for the subsequent modification of one or more of the queries, q.

Finally, the combination queries determined in each cycle of the algorithm constitute the nodes for the next cycle, with the messages to be broadcast remaining the same as initially created. The algorithm returns the combination query (or queries) that contain the greatest number of data items common to the input query S.

3.4   Step 3 – Constraint Matching

A successful query match also requires a satisfactory match between the constraints in S and those in $q \in Q$. Each query is optionally defined with a set of constraints as indicated in Eq. (1) and Eq. (2). For a successful constraint match, or rather a *constraint feasible solution*, the constraints in the supplied query S, must be compatible with the constraints in the matching query $q \in Q$. Constraints that are compatible indicate that the constraints in S will satisfy the corresponding constraints in $q \in Q$. This point is clarified with the following example: If a query S contains a negotiation constraint, *price* < $20.00 and a matching query $q \in Q$ contains a corresponding constraint, *price* = $10.00, then if S is considered an information request and $q \in Q$ an information offer, then these particular constraints are compatible.

The challenge that arises with the constraint matching process is to evaluate not only the semantics of the constraints, but the quantitative aspects as well. There are no actual data values to evaluate the constraints during the match process, and so the effect that the operators have on these data items cannot be readily identified. Therefore a new method to evaluate the constraints must be devised. This algorithm assesses the compatibility of the constraints provided in a query S and a matching query $q \in Q$. The goal of the algorithm is to ascertain if the constraints provided in the matching queries are compatible with each other, that is, are the variables/data items of the same domain, and if so, will the data values satisfy each other. In doing so, *truth tables* are utilized to evaluate matching constraints, which is discussed in greater detail in the following.

Each constraint provided in a query consists of a data item / negotiation attribute i, a comparison operator from the set $\{=, <, >\}$, and a data item / literal value v. Therefore, for each constraint in S and in $q \in Q$, establish all the possible constraint variations given the set of comparison operators. For example, given a constraint, *price* < 20, then the variations of this constraint include *price* = 20, and *price* > 20. In the first step of the algorithm, given the set of constraints in S and in q, the matrix V is created to consist of all the provided constraints and their variations. This matrix V is denoted as the *matrix of assertions*. Table 4-1 illustrates a simple example of the construction of a matrix V, given three constraints; q constraints: $x = 1$, $y = 4$, and S constraints: $x < 5$.

Table 4-5. Table of Assertions for Constraint Matching Algorithm

	Constraint Number		
	$x = 1$	$y = 4$	$x = 5$
Variation Number	$x < 1$	$y < 4$	$x < 5$
	$x > 1$	$y > 4$	$x > 5$

In the second step of the algorithm, all combinations of the assertions in V are determined and their compatibility assessed. Accordingly, the number of combinations to be evaluated is determined by the following formula: 3^n, where n is the total number of constraints, which is the sum of the number of constraints in S and those in $q \in Q$. For each combination of the constraints the compatibility is determined along with the validity of the constraint, when compared with the provided constraints in S and in q. That is, a combination constraint is *true* if it is compatible, and if the constraints in the combination match the original constraints (See Table 4-2).

Table 4-6. Compatibility and Truth Table for Constraint Matching Algorithm

Constraint Combination			Compatible	S	q
$x = 1$	$y = 4$	$x = 5$	No		
$x = 1$	$y = 4$	$x < 5$	Yes	T	T
$x = 1$	$y = 4$	$x > 5$	No		
...	...	...	...	...	...
$x > 1$	$y > 1$	$x > 5$	Yes	F	F

Comparing $y = 4$ and $x < 5$ to $x = 1$, highlights the fact that this constraint combination is compatible since (1) $x = 1$, does satisfy $x < 5$, and (2) $y = 4$ and $x = 1$ are compatible. This latter argument requires elaboration. By default, constraints in different domains are compatible, and since x and y are different domains then $y = 4$ and $x = 1$ are compatible. Also, this combination constraint is true for each constraint in S and $q \in Q$, since each of the constraints in the combination match the originally provided constraints.

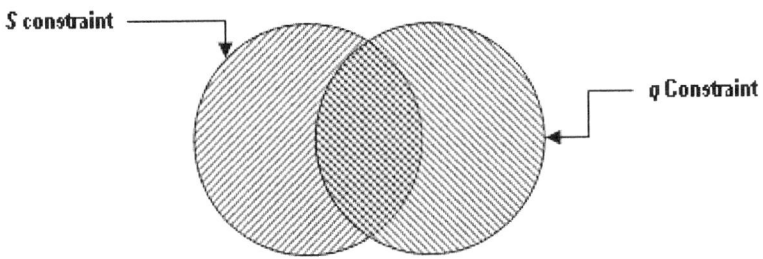

S constraint

q Constraint

Figure 4-3. Determination of the Type of Constraint Match

The compilation of the results found in Table 4-6 reveal the numbers of *true/true* (*TT*), *true/false* (*TF*) and *false/true* (*FT*) results for the given set of constraints in S and $q \in Q$. A *true/true* result corresponds to the intersection of both regions in Fig. 4-3, whereas a *true/false* corresponds to the region bounded by S constraint, and conversely a *false/true* is bounded by q constraint in Fig. 4-3. A *false/false* result can also be determined, which is the complement of $S_{constraint} \cup q_{constraint}$, but this is discarded since this simply indicates that the constraints do not match. It is necessary to determine how the constraints match and so emphasis is placed on the results that provide such information. Therefore, the *TT*, *TF* and *FT* results are classified according to the aforementioned *exact, superset/subset,* and *intersect* classification described in Section 3.1. Where the compiled results from Table 4-2 indicate a *TT* quantity greater than zero, with the *TF* and *FT* equal to zero, then an exact match between the constraints has been identified. This is summarized Table 4-3:

Table 4-7. Classification of Constraint Match Results

	TT	TF	FT
Exact	> 0	= 0	= 0
Superset	> 0	> 0	= 0
Subset	> 0	= 0	> 0
Intersect	> 0	> 0	> 0

Algorithm 3 (*Constraint Match*) in Table 4-8 determines the constraint feasibility of a query S and a matching query $q \in Q$.

Table 4-8. **Algorithm 3**: *Constraint Matching* (S^C, q^C)

Let S^C: The set of constraints associated with S.

Let q^C: The set of constraints associated with q.

Let A: the current assertion

Let V: The set of all assertions corresponding to the constraints in S^C and q^C.

Let Initialize(A, B): Create a matrix of assertions from the constraints A and B. V is a two dimensional array of constraint variations.

Let Op: The set of operators $\{=, <, >\}$

Let evaluate(A, B): Assess the truth value of A and B.

Let accumulate(A, B): Sum AB, where A and B can be T or F. So TT = TT + 1 if A is T and B is T. Perform also for TF and FT.

Let Compatible(A, B): Determine if B is compatible with the current set of assertions in A.

$TT \leftarrow \varnothing$
$TF \leftarrow \varnothing$
$FT \leftarrow \varnothing$
$A \leftarrow \varnothing$
$V \leftarrow Initialize(S^C, q^C)$
If $count(S^C \cup q^C) \neq 0$
For $v = 1$ to $count(Op)$
    $Match\ (A, V, S^C, q^C, 1, v)$
End-For
End-If
Function $Match\ (A, V, S^C, q^C, u, v)$
If $Compatible(A, V[u][v])$
  $A[u] \leftarrow V[u][v]$
  If $u = count(S^C \cup q^C)$
accumulate $(evaluate(S^C, A), evaluate(q^C, A))$
Else
For $v = 1$ to $count(Op)$
    $Match\ (A, V, S^C, q^C, u + 1, v)$
  End-For
End-If
End-If
End-Function

Definition 5 and Definition 6 establish the criteria for the constraint feasible solution of a query S and matching query $q \in Q$, or matching combination query $\left(\bigcup_i q_i \right)$.

Definition 5:

$$q \cap S \in CF \Rightarrow \forall S^C, \exists q^C \in Q^C \text{ such that } q^C \cap S^C \neq \varnothing$$

The match of a query S and a query $q \in Q$ is constraint feasible if the constraints in S and q are compatible.

Definition 6:

$$\left(\bigcup_{i} q_i\right) \cap S \in CF \Rightarrow \forall\, S^C, \exists\, q^C \in Q^C, \forall\left(\bigcup_{i} q_i^{C}\right), \text{ such that } \left(\bigcup_{i} q_i^{C}\right) \cap S^C \neq \varnothing$$

The match of a combination query $\left(\bigcup_{i} q_i\right)$ and query S is constraint feasible, if the constraints in the S and in each query q_i are compatible.

4. QUERY ALLOCATION: ASSIGN QUERIES TO WINNING EXPORT DATABASES

Once a satisfactory match has been found, then the query S is allocated to the corresponding export database of the matching query $q \in Q$. It is trivial if S matches a single $q \in Q$, but is non-trivial if multiple queries, $q \in Q$ are a satisfactory match for S. The non-trivial case assumes that the queries $q \in Q$ are similarly item, join and constraint feasible and they can be substituted for each other to provide a single, equivalent satisfactory match for S. It is assumed in this non-trivial case that S corresponds to a subscription query, and conversely $q \in Q$ corresponds to a publication query, and so to identify a single query will require the use of decision rules. The list below provides four decision criteria which can be specified as actions during query formulation. Recall that multiple actions can be specified in a query, and so these decision criteria can be specified in any combination; grouped all together, or only a single criterion specified.

Heuristic: *First-Come, First-Serve and Last-Come First-Serve* – uses the system-defined timestamp of each query to select a winner. In First-Come First-Serve, the query with the oldest timestamp, i.e., the query that has been registered with the Blackboard for the greatest amount of time is selected. The assumption here is that the associated export database will be reliable. In Last-Come First-Serve the query with the most recent timestamp, i.e., the query that has been registered with the Blackboard for the least amount of time is selected. The assumption here is that the associated export database will have current data.

Network Performance – determines the geographical location of the export databases, assuming that further distances contribute to network latency, and chooses the export database that is in closer proximity to its location. This requires that the Blackboard shell has the functionality, or is connected to resources that can assess the geographical location of other systems in the TSCM.

Past History – the export database that is popular, that is, where it has frequently provided answers in other previous matching sessions will be chosen over an export database that has not been similarly prolific. Moreover, if the export database is reliable, that is, if the export database has significantly greater success than not, in providing answers in previous matching sessions. This requires that the Blackboard shell maintain the history of past sessions, such that these statistics can be determined.

Preferred Organizations – the selected export database will be chosen from a list of preferred export databases that have been specified during query formulation. It may be desired to restrict the allocation to a specific export database, say for example, government, military or academic export databases. In this respect, the Blackboard must provide a mechanism, or is connected to a mechanism that authenticates and classifies the export databases that participate in the TSCM.

On the other hand, if multiple equivalent subscription queries $q \in Q$ are found for a supplied publication query S, then generally no decision rules are required to choose a "winner," since the subscription queries match the publication query. The export database will therefore service each subscription query. However, these decision criteria are still provided during query formulation, and so can be specified during the construction of a publication query. Accordingly, the Blackboard will filter the subscription queries as required.

In the event that actions are not included in queries that match each other, then the Blackboard automatically selects a winning match from the available decision criteria. If the publication query dominates and multiple subscriptions queries are found, then the Blackboard may choose to filter, or stagger the results to an acceptable number, rather than load the export database with an excessive number of queries. If the subscription query dominates, then the Blackboard may rank the publication queries to provide a result of increased "quality". If the Blackboard still cannot determine an acceptable solution then it will seek manual input to choose an appropriate solution.

5.   QUERY EXECUTION: OBTAINING RESULTS FROM THE EXPORT DATABASE

The execution of the query on the export databases, which is achieved through the particular architecture discussed in Chapter 5, constitutes the final phase of query processing in the TSCM. The supplied query is delivered to the winning export database shell as described in the previous section, where it is transformed from Extended Metadatabase Query Language (exMQL) format to its equivalent Structured Query Language (SQL) representation for execution on the export database. The query is processed and the results returned from the export database are then transformed into an exMQL message and delivered to the Blackboard, where it is forwarded to the initiator of the supplied query. The query execution process is discussed in greater detail in Chapters 5 and 6.

6.   A SUMMARY OF THE QUERY MATCHING PROCESS

The query matching process is summarized in the following text, and as illustrated in Fig. 4-4. A query S that is an exact match of a query $q \in Q$, or if S is a subset of $q \in Q$ then $q \in Q$ (See Section 3.2) is automatically considered item feasible (IF) and join feasible (JF), and so we continue onwards to test for the constraint feasibility (CF) of the match.

If the query S otherwise matches the query $q \in Q$, i.e. if S is a superset of, or intersects $q \in Q$, then the match algorithm enters into a second stage of matching (See Section 3.3) to determine combinations of these results $\bigcup_i q_i$, which are again compared with S to determine their item and join feasibility. If $q \in Q$ or $\bigcup_i q_i$ is not item feasible then the query matching algorithm terminates.

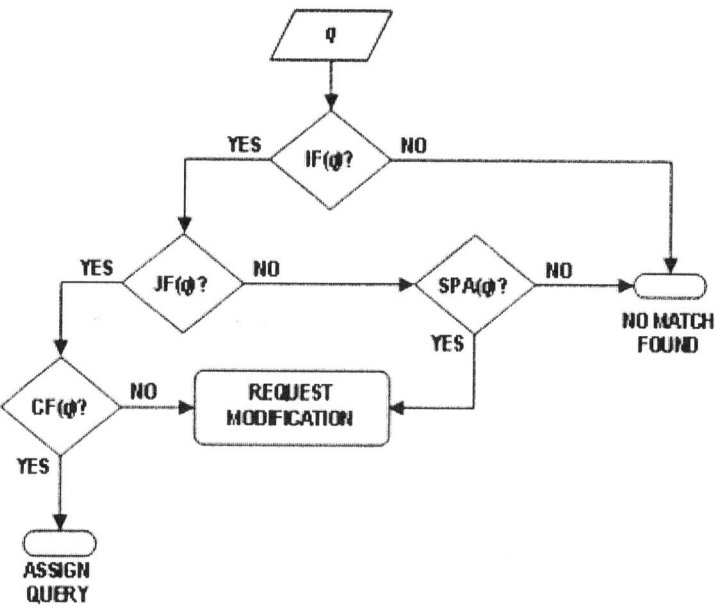

Figure 4-4. The Evaluation of a Combination Match Evaluation

If $\bigcup_i q_i$ is join feasible, which implies that the data items are logically connected and that a common item exists in all queries, then $\bigcup_i q_i$ is tested for constraint feasibility. In the event that $\bigcup_i q_i$ is not join feasible, then $\bigcup_i q_i$ is evaluated with the Shortest Path Algorithm (*SPA*) (Cheung 1991). If the SPA determines a solution for $\bigcup_i q_i$ then it is necessary to request the inclusion of the missing items found by the *SPA* before $\bigcup_i q_i$ is considered join feasible. If the *SPA* cannot determine the join feasibility of $\bigcup_i q_i$ then it indicates that the individual queries cannot be logically connected given the information in the Metadatabase, and therefore the query matching algorithm is terminated.

The query S is assigned to the corresponding export database of $q \in Q$, or the export databases of $\bigcup_i q_i$ if these are constraint feasible. In the event $q \in Q$ or $\bigcup_i q_i$ are not constraint feasible then it is necessary to request the modification of the constraints in the appropriate queries.

7. THE ADVANTAGES OF THE NEW EXECUTION METHODS WHEN COMPARED WITH TRADITIONAL APPROACHES

The new execution methods provide improvements for global query in distributed database systems, specifically in the areas of database autonomy, heterogeneity and scalability as highlighted in the sub-sections that follow. The introduction of the publication queries to the global query regime, as facilitated by export databases, and the algorithms that support the matching of these queries with subscription queries on the Blackboard contributes to the advantages of the TSCM over the traditional methods of global query.

7.1 Database Autonomy

By virtue of its dependence on the Metadatabase, the TSCM inherits the contributions in autonomy, open architectures and extensibility already realized in the original research; but it also expands on these areas significantly in its own right. In the original research the schemata of the distributed database systems are consolidated into a global information model (See Chapter 2) that resolves the semantic heterogeneities that exists among the individual schemata. The application of the global information model on the federation differs from traditional approaches, in that the global information model is not imposed on each component database systems, rather it works in concert with the local schemata. In fact, the schemata of the local databases remain unchanged when associated with the Metadatabase therefore contributing to its relatively greater autonomy.

The global information model (See Fig. 2-4) is implemented as a regular database schema, and the local data models and their attendant functional (operating, decision and business rules) constructs are essentially tuples in the underlying database system. Modifications to the global information model, such as the addition of new local schemas, or the update or deletion of existing local schemas are made using insert, update and delete commands in MQL, which are equivalent to the commands found in standard SQL.

The TSCM extend the autonomy of the databases participating Metadatabase-enabled global query, by offering the ability to connect and disconnect from global query infrastructure at will, yet retaining the membership of the local data model in the Metadatabase. In traditional global query systems, including the Metadatabase, a distributed database is always available for global database query. The databases are subservient to the global query authority, and cannot control when and how their data resources are utilized, unless the local data model is removed entirely from the global query infrastructure. In the Metadatabase context, this essentially requires the deletion of tuples from the Metadatabase, but in traditional systems the effort may be a significant undertaking. To re-connect to the global query architecture, the local schema must enter into the initial registration phase once again, which can be a significant undertaking. The TSCM on the other hand separates the registration mechanism from the global query architecture, as represented by the Metadatabase and Blackboard respectively. Furthermore, this new approach is supported by the new publish/subscribe mechanism facilitated by publication queries and subscription queries respectively. Therefore, a local database participates in global query *only* when the data to be shared is made public, by submitting queries to the Blackboard. Otherwise, the local database remains a part of the global query architecture, but does not participate in it.

7.2   Database Heterogeneity

In traditional global query, the component databases are subject to the authority of the database management system, and so their participation in global query is unconditional. Moreover, the DBMS imposes the global query language and the global schema on the component databases. The Metadatabase technology affords participating databases the opportunity to maintain a heterogeneous local schema, while still participating in global query. The Metadatabase transforms all global queries from the global query format to an equivalent local query format via ROPE, which are software shells that encapsulate the databases (Babin 1993). The TSCM therefore inherits this functionality but extends the heterogeneity of a local database in the Metadatabase architecture in two ways. First, all resources in the TSCM and beyond the boundaries of an enterprise database exist in the global scope. The global schema, the export database schema, query language, and data values are all global defined. The enterprise database monitor (See Chapter 5) has the responsibility of converting the local data values and attributes to their equivalent global representation. Second, MQL is extended to include the concept of rules, which include constraints that qualify the data items, and actions that additionally assess the best results returned from global query. The opportunity to declare constraints at the query level (See Section 2) provides a degree of extensibility, and heterogeneity that was necessary but until now has not been realized in the Metadatabase architecture.

7.3   Integration Scalability and Open Architectures

Integration scalability pertains to the ability of the distributed database management systems to add increasingly greater numbers of databases without loss of functionality and performance, but rather to take full advantage of the available resources. Scalability was not a significant barrier to functionality in traditional DBMSs, for the simple fact the numbers of databases included in a database integration framework was small. But, as the database environment grows, which is more evident in today's enterprise infrastructure, and Internet-facilitated industrial exchanges, then the ability to manage a global query in these infrastructures using traditional methods is impossible, and so new methods are necessary to support this.

The Metadatabase has already provided a compelling mechanism to improve the scalability and openness of global query, via the methods provided to add new databases to the global data model (Hsu, Bouziane et al. 1991). The Metadatabase approach also can be installed on standard relational database technology, and so the scalability of the global information model, and therefore the integration scalability are limited only by the capabilities of the hardware and software.

The new methods of the TSCM extend the scalability and maintain the openness of the Metadatabase architecture. Export database shells facilitate the addition of diverse database systems and alternative data sources as well, if necessary. The primary effort required in this regard, is the development of *wrappers* required to retrieve the data from the enterprise databases, and transform the resident data from the native format to the global format. These export databases therefore can submit any number of queries to the Blackboard, to take part in query matching. Consequently, the scalability of the Blackboard is limited by the capabilities of the underlying database hardware and software. The openness of the Blackboard and therefore the TSCM is limited by the number of wrappers provided to integrate the enterprise databases.

Chapter 5

THE ARCHITECTURAL COMPONENTS OF THE TWO-STAGE COLLABORATION MODEL

1.   OVERVIEW

This chapter describes the architectural components that are required to support the algorithms described in the previous chapter, and in general to actualize the TSCM. As previously indicated, the global query methods implement the functionality of the Blackboard, which serves as the hub of collaboration in the TSCM. The Metadatabase maintains the global data model and supports the Blackboard in instances where additional semantic information is required during query matching. An enterprise database participating in the TSCM is represented by an export database shell, which contains an export database and additional apparatus to facilitate the information sharing within the TSCM. These components are connected to each other via a messaging protocol, combined with exMQL. The message protocol provides the transport for messages between the components of the TSCM, and encapsulates the exMQL commands necessary to manipulate queries at the Blackboard. Finally, the exMGQS facilitates the construction of queries, both subscription and publication queries; in addition to monitoring the status of the query matching process at the Blackboard. These components are explored in greater detail in the sections that follow.

2. THE PROTOTYPE STRUCTURE OF THE BLACKBOARD

The Blackboard shell (See Fig. 2-1), abbreviated Blackboard, is a software shell that encapsulates the query database and rulebase as well as additional components necessary for query management, processing and optimization. The query database, which maintains the list of queries, and rulebase, which maintains the constraints associated with the queries are implemented on a standard relational database management system (RDBMS) that is extended by the implementation of the algorithms described in the previous chapter, as well as the new query language exMQL. In this regard, the RDBMS is denoted as the **Blackboard Database Management System (BDBMS)**. The BDBMS therefore implements the algorithms in Chapter 4 by using the procedural language facility (e.g. PL/SQL in Oracle, and PL/pgSQL in PostgreSQL) of the underlying RDBMS. The remaining software components of the Blackboard include: the Network Monitor, Message Processor, and Result Integrator.

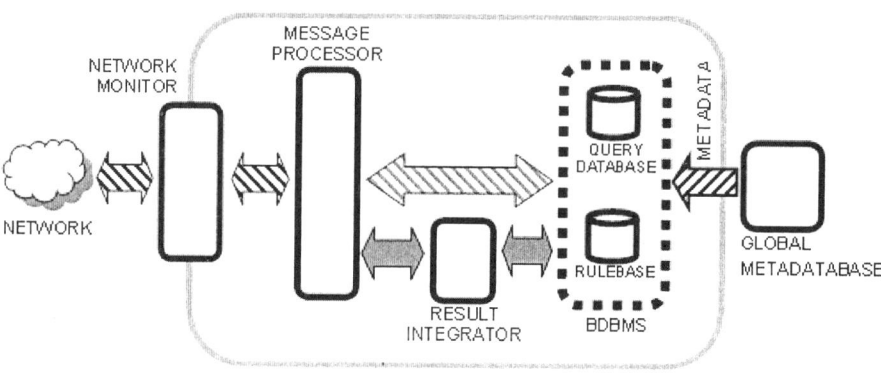

Figure 5-1. Blackboard Prototype Architecture

The **Message Processor** is used primarily to transform exMQL queries that are to be added to the Blackboard database to an equivalent series of SQL (Structured Query Language) INSERT statements. Subsequent to the query matching process, if a matching query is not found, the supplied query is added to the Blackboard database. The message processor therefore transforms the supplied query into a series of INSERT statements, organized to respect dependency constraints. This transaction is described in greater detail in Chapter 6.

The results returned from the Blackboard database include the identification of the export database(s) that satisfy the supplied query, along with the corresponding data items and constraints. Accordingly, these database results are converted to their equivalent message representation, and are directed to the Network Monitor for additional processing.

The **Network Monitor** directs all communication to the appropriate targets. It listens for all incoming query messages and redirects them to the Message Processor for further processing as indicated above. In this regard, the Network Monitor removes the message envelope and forwards the message body to the Message Processor. For outgoing messages, such as notifications sent to export databases matching the supplied query, the Network Monitor transforms the matching data items and constraints, and encapsulates this content in a message envelope for delivery to the affected export databases. In the event that, multiple queries must be integrated to satisfy the supplied query, which corresponds to a combination match, then the Network Monitor maintains a database of the notified export databases, and the pending integration requirement, and waits for responses from them. When all results are retrieved from the affected export databases, they are directed to the Result Integrator for consolidation into a single result. The Network Monitor uses the knowledge of queries stored in the Blackboard database (e.g. IP addresses) to forward outgoing messages and query results to their required destinations.

The primary responsibility of the **Result Integrator** is the integration of results from a combination match. The Result Integrator consolidates the actual query results (not the query metadata) from the corresponding export databases, according to the data supplied by the BDBMS. A combination match provides the necessary integration requirements for the Result Integrator; the involved data items determine the affected export databases, while the necessary joins that produce the match dictate how the Result Integrator must combine the results returned from these databases. The combined results are then directed to the Message Processor and then on to the Network Monitor to be forwarded to the supplier of the initial query.

The **Global Metadatabase** maintains the global data model and is the central authority to which Local Metadatabases subscribe (See Chapter 5). As described in Chapter 5, the Metadatabase provides an integrated model of global metadata, which also considers global knowledge such as operating and business rules corresponding to a local or enterprise database. For its role in the TSCM, the Metadatabase is primarily used for this global knowledge, and the facility to transform global attributes and values, into local attributes and values, and vice versa. It is also used for the evaluation of combination queries in the combination algorithm depicted in Table 4-3

88

(See Chapter 4 for additional details), where the combination of disparate queries is determined to be feasible if the Shortest Path Algorithm returns a result. Finally, as a component of the exMGQS the Metadatabase also contributes to the construction of queries (See Section 4).

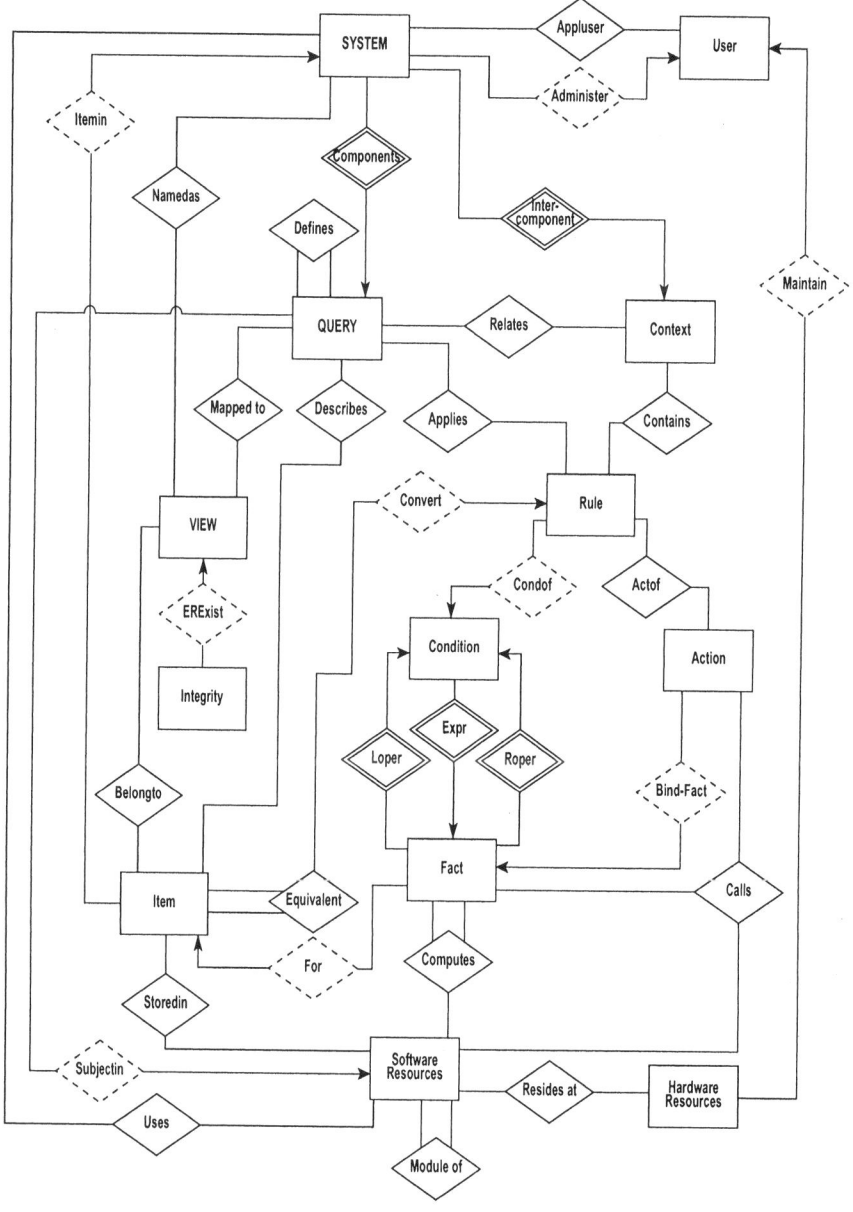

Figure 5-2. Conceptual Structure of the Blackboard Database

The conceptual structure of the Blackboard database is derived from the Global Information Resources Dictionary (GIRD), which is also the conceptual structure of the Metadatabase (See Chapter 2). However, the requirements of the GIRD are relaxed for the purposes of the Blackboard database, and so a number of the elements of the GIRD are unused but are retained in the information model for possible future expansion. In this regard, this version of the GIRD is denoted as the Blackboard schema, which conceptually constitutes two distinct database schemas and can be implemented as such, but as illustrated in Fig. 5-2 and implemented in this research (See Appendix B) they are contained in a single structural model.

2.1   The Conceptual Structure of the Query Database

The main changes to the GIRD to satisfy the requirements of the Blackboard schema are the SYSTEM, QUERY, and VIEW meta-entities, which replace the APPLICATION, SUBJECT and ENTREL meta-entities. The remaining meta-entities, and meta-relationships, that is the Functional Relationships (FR), Mandatory Relationships (MR) and Plural Relationships (PR) that connect them, retain their original definitions as outlined in (Bouziane 1991; Hsu, Bouziane et al. 1991), with minor extensions. The relevant changes are clarified in the list below.

The SYSTEM meta-entity identifies the enterprise databases that are currently participating in global query, and accordingly the export database shell that represent the local enterprise. Each export database shell is defined by a unique identifier, which is determined at design-time when the local data model is integrated into the Metadatabase. However, this is not made available to the global Blackboard unless a query has been submitted to the Blackboard by the export database.

The QUERY meta-entity identifies the queries submitted by the export database. Each query submitted to the Blackboard is unique, and is associated with a unique identifier that is assigned at run-time. A timestamp attribute is generated automatically when the query is received at the Blackboard. The timestamp is primarily used for breaking ties, as discussed in Chapter 4, but is also used to remove queries from the query database after a user-defined or system-enforced expiration date and time. The related COMPONENTS meta-MR associates queries with a particular export database (SYSTEM), and upholds existence and dependency constraints by deleting these corresponding queries if the export database is removed entirely from the Blackboard. This will occur if no queries owned by the export database are resident at the Blackboard.

The VIEW meta-entity, in its currently implemented form is an alias for the QUERY meta-entity, and so displays the same list of data items described in a query. The complete implementation of a query may have multiple views, which is analogous to the traditional definition of a database *view*. Indeed, the conceptual model provides this opportunity, since an export database can submit more than one query to the Blackboard. Therefore, it is possible for the queries to contain common items, which then implies that the unique identifiers of the data items are shared. It is important to note that there cannot be multiple instances of unique identifiers in the query database.

The ITEM meta-entity remains unchanged from its original definition (Cheung 1991), and represents the data items specified in each query. The related BELONGTO meta-PR associates data items to a specific VIEW, and the DESCRIBES meta-PR specifies the data items that belong to each QUERY.

2.2   The Conceptual Structure of the Rulebase

The rulebase maintains its original definitions as described in (Bouziane 1991), although the context in which it is used has changed. In the original definition, the RULE meta-entity consolidated the decision, business and operating rules in the global data model. These rules took the form, IF *condition* THEN *action*, and only operated on the data items in the Metadatabase. In its new context, the RULE meta-entity consolidates the various constraint types discussed in Chapter 4, and actions as defined in a query. Consequently, the RULE meta-entity is comprised of the CONDITION, ACTION meta-entities, and the additional meta-plural relationships necessary to support the abstraction of the rules (See Fig. 5-2).

The general syntax of a rule is based on the Event-Condition-Action (ECA) grammar described in (Babin 1993). The ECA paradigm suggests that given the occurrence of an event, and the positive assertion of its condition(s), the corresponding action(s) should be executed. Now, the event in question always refers to the successful match of data items at the Blackboard, regardless of the class of match as specified in Chapter 4, although generally the default action on an exact match will always deliver the results to the corresponding recipient. As with the constraints in a query, the actions in a rule can also be defined during query construction.

As discussed in Chapter 4, a constraint takes the form of an operation between an attribute or data item, and literal value in the case of negotiation and selection constraints respectively, and between data items in the case of join constraints. This is depicted in Fig. 5-2 by the CONDITION meta-entity, which abstracts the negotiation, selection and join constraints; while the FACT meta-entity provides additional details about the components of this abstraction.

The implemented functionality of the Blackboard is limited to the scope of meta-entities and the supporting meta-relations that are specifically discussed in this section, but additional details on the remaining elements of the rulebase model can be found in (Bouziane 1991).

3. THE PROTOTYPE STRUCTURE OF THE EXPORT DATABASE SHELL

Figure 5-3 illustrates the elements of the export database shell, which encapsulates the export database and additional elements necessary to support the ability of the database to share information in the TSCM. The export database also maintains the globally defined data and attributes of the local equivalents found in the enterprise databases, which it represents. Moreover, the schema of the export database is defined by the data items contained in the publication queries that are issued via the exMGQS. A standard relational database system is used to implement the export database, and accordingly the native query language is utilized for accessing the database. Finally, the remaining software components of the export database shell include the Network Monitor and Message Processor.

The **Network Monitor** and **Message Processor** provide similar functionality as described in Section 2. The Network Monitor listens for incoming query execution requests from the Blackboard, and passes these on to the Message Processor for additional processing. It strips the query execution request of its message envelope and submits the message body to the Message Processor. The Message Processor transforms all incoming messages queries into their equivalent SQL representation and submits it to the Export Database Management System (EDBMS) for processing. Conversely, the Message Processor converts the outgoing query results from the EDBMS into their messaging format, to which the Network Monitor adds the message envelope for delivery to the Blackboard.

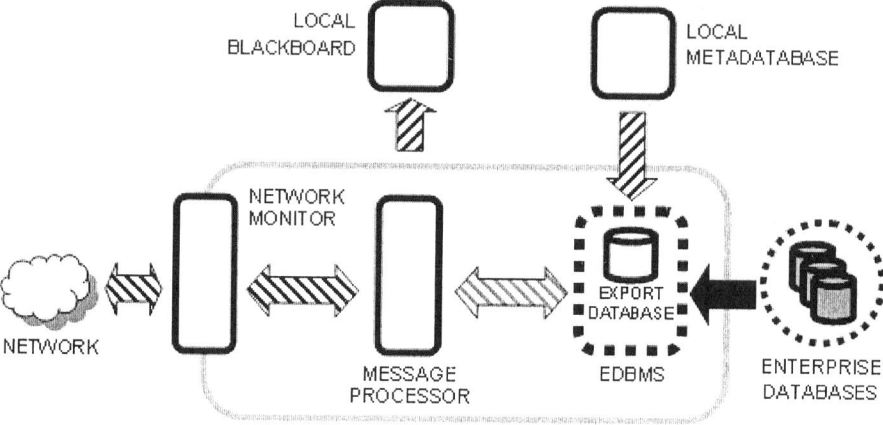

Figure 5-3. Prototype Structure of the Export Database Shell

The **Export Database** is the repository of data corresponding to publication queries issued via the exMGQS. This data is obtained from the enterprise database(s) that exist in the local domain, and are updated through an **enterprise database monitor**, which is unique for each enterprise database. This design is provided to facilitate the open architecture of the TSCM, and particularly to work in concert with the heterogeneous systems that the TSCM will no doubt encounter. Moreover, if the enterprise databases are shielded from public view by software or hardware-based firewalls, then the export database provides the opportunity for these enterprise databases to still participate in the TSCM.

To populate the export database with data corresponding to a publication query, however, still requires the export database shell to have access to the enterprise databases. How this is implemented, and how it is managed is the responsibility of the local domain, although multiple alternatives are possible in the TSCM design. The export database shell can be installed in front of the firewall and connected to the enterprise databases via a secured TCP port. On the other hand, the export database can be connected behind the firewall, which would require it to communicate through an open port on the firewall. We defer the resolution of these issues for a future design of the TSCM.

As stated earlier, the export database is implemented on a standard relational database, and so all incoming queries from the Message Processor are transformed to the native language of the export database, which in the current design will be SQL queries. The **Export Database Management**

System implements the interface and data management facilities of the export database.

The **Local Metadatabase** in the current implementation facilitates the query transformation process by converting the local data values retrieved from the enterprise database into their global equivalent when populating the export database. In its minimum implementation it serves as a reference table that provides a mapping of local attributes to global attributes, and the necessary conversion factors to go from local values to global values. In the full implementation it is an exact copy of the Global Metadatabase, and captures the complete knowledge, which is the business, decision and operation rules of all enterprise databases participating in the TSCM. Furthermore, the Local Metadatabase works in concert with the Local Blackboard when the export database shell participates in a peer-to-peer manner with other export database shells.

The **Local Blackboard** facilitates peer-to-peer global query, where each export database shell can initiate a global query session directly with other export database shells. The initiating export database shell in this context will operate in a manner analogous to Global Blackboard, but exists outside the purview of the central Global Blackboard. In this role the export database shell functions exactly as described in Section 2, however the discussion of this peer-to-peer functionality is beyond the scope of this research.

4. THE PROTOTYPE STRUCTURE OF THE EXTENDED METADATABASE GLOBAL QUERY SYSTEM

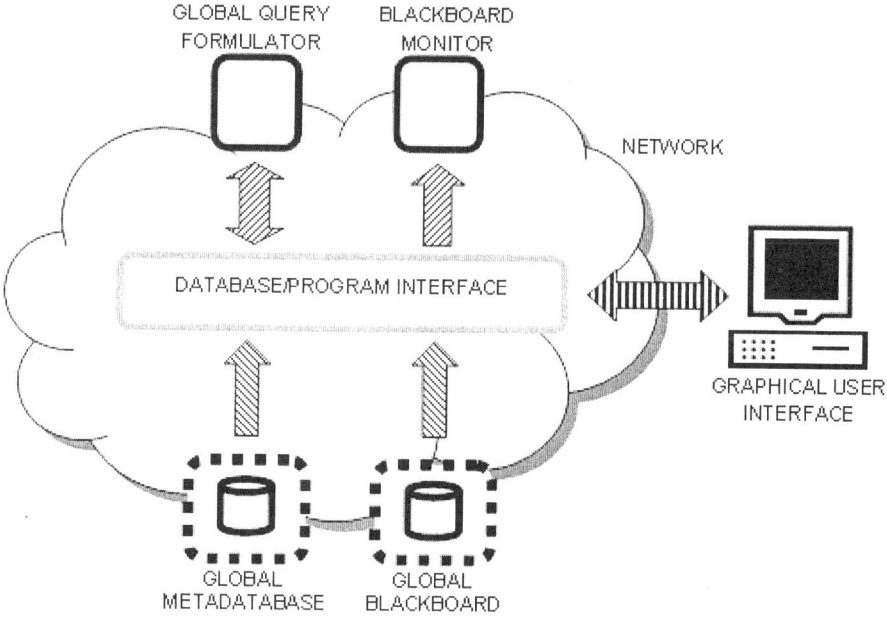

Figure 5-4. The Architecture of the Extended Metadatabase Global Query System

The extended Metadatabase Global Query System (exMGQS) extends the original implementation of the GQS (Babin 1993; Cheung and Hsu 1996) primarily through the addition of the Blackboard as a data source for query formulation, as well as the addition of the new context applied to queries, notably subscription and publication queries (See Fig. 5-4). Moreover, the new rule processing methods are added, which previously were not addressed at this level of the GQS design, and so the interface and functionality are modified to reflect these changes. The exMGQS therefore consists of the components necessary to facilitate the construction of queries, and so is not simply a graphical user interface; most importantly it combines a Global Query Formulator to provide online-assistance during query formulation. A Blackboard Monitor is also provided to display the status of the query matching processes to users of the exMGQS, who gain visual access through the graphical user interface.

The **Global Query Formulator** is an interactive tool that facilitates the construction and manipulation of queries (See Section 5) in the exMGQS. It provides the underlying methods required to interactively navigate the Blackboard and Metadatabase. The *vertical traversal* of the Metadatabase directs query formulation in a path that leads from a selected APPLICATION to its component data ITEMs. Along the path, the navigation would have revealed the component SUBJECT and ENTITY-RELATIONSHIPS. Similarly, when vertically navigating the Blackboard, the Global Query Formulator reveals the ITEMs and QUERY that belong to a selected SYSTEM (export database). Conversely, the original research (Cheung 1991) also describes a *horizontal traversal* method, where navigating the Metadatabase reveals the adjacent meta-entities (OE) and meta-plural relationships (PR) when an OE/PR is selected in the Metadatabase. This process however cannot be implemented for the Blackboard since the common elements across export databases are the data items alone. In fact, the matching algorithms in Chapter 4 provide this functionality; by pivoting around the provided data items in a query we are able to identify complementary queries.

During query construction, the Query Formulator does the following: (1) validates the query, (2) detects and notifies the user if the data items and constraints are semantically inconsistent, if they belong to mismatched domains, or if they have conflicting data formats. The result of the query formulation process is therefore a semantically consistent and validated query, which can then be submitted directly to the Blackboard.

The **Blackboard Monitor** is activated when a query has been added to the Blackboard, and so provides updates on the performance of the queries owned by each export database.

The **Graphical User Interface**, which is described in further detail in Chapter 6 is implemented using basic HTML and JavaScript programming, and is accessible from a standard Internet browser. The content of the GUI is provided by the Blackboard and Metadatabase, through the database interfaces illustrated in Fig. 5-4.

5.   EXTENDED MQL: A QUERY LANGUAGE FOR THE TSCM

The Extended Metadatabase Query Language (exMQL) is designed to provide a uniform query format for the various query operations that are required in the TSCM. The structure is derived from the original MQL specification in (Cheung 1991), and therefore is also based on the TSER representation method. It differs distinctly from the original MQL however, due to the new publication method and to the new rule specification to the query language. The full syntax specification of exMQL is illustrated in Figs. 5-5 to 5-15, and uses an alternative Backus-Naur Format (BNF) described in (Babin 2004). A corresponding XML representation is also provided in Appendix A. In particular, exMQL:

- Supports queries requiring joins of data from different export databases. During the match process, the Blackboard will consult the Metadatabase to determine if the query can be joined on the data items.
- Uses familiar names for the data items in queries. The Metadatabase and Blackboard utilize the *itemcode*, a unique internal identifier used for all data items in both databases.
- Minimizes technical details expected of users for the global query formulation, while supporting the above functionalities (e.g., the physical locations, local names, and implicit join conditions).

In Fig. 5-5 to 5-15, the GET and PUT commands specify a subscription query (information request) and publication query (information offer), respectively. Both commands are followed by a space-delimited list of data items for retrieval (subscription) or sharing (publication), respectively as represented by the ITEMs category. At least one data item must be provided in a query, which in addition to the GET or PUT command. These are the minimum requirements for a global query in the TSCM.

The FOR command specifies constraints on the data items specified in the query, as well as constraints on the query in general. As specified in Chapter 4, three classes of constraints are considered: selection conditions (SC), join conditions (JC) and negotiation conditions (NC). These conditions serve two functions: (1) to be used in the evaluation of a match (See Chapter 4), and (2) to be used in a manner analogous to the WHERE command in traditional SQL.

- `<QUERY> ::= <COMMAND> <ITEMS> *['FOR' <CONDITIONS>]* *['DO' <ACTIONS>]* ;`

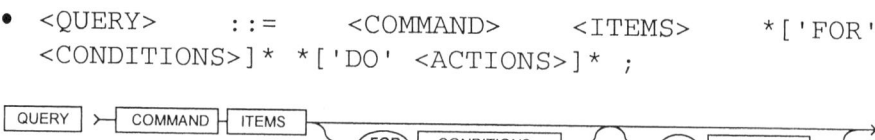

Figure 5-5. exMQL QUERY Clause

- `<ITEMS> ::= /[ item || ',' ]/ ;`

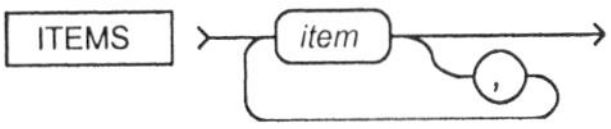

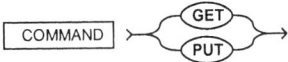

Figure 5-6. exMQL ITEMS Clause

- `<COMMAND> ::= 'GET' | 'PUT' ;`

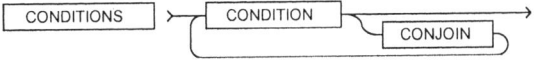

Figure 5-7. exMQL QUERY COMMAND options

- `<CONDITIONS> ::= /[ <CONDITION> || <CONJOIN> ]/;`

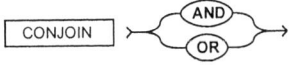

Figure 5-8. exMQL CONDITIONS Clause

- `<CONJOIN> ::= 'AND' | 'OR' ;`

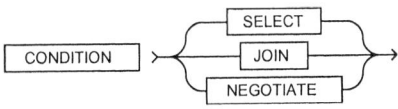

Figure 5-9. exMQL CONJOIN options

- `<CONDITION> ::= <SELECT> | <JOIN> | <NEGOTIATE> ;`

Figure 5-10. exMQL CONDITION options

- `<SELECTION> ::= item <BOUND> value ;`

Figure 5-11. exMQL SELECTION Clause

- `<JOIN> ::= item <BOUND> item ;`

Figure 5-12. exMQL JOIN Clause

- `<NEGOTIATE> ::= attribute <BOUND> value ;`

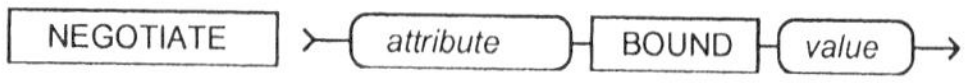

Figure 5-13. exMQL NEGOTIATE Clause

- `<BOUND> ::= '<>' | '=' | '<' | '>' | '<=' | '>=';`

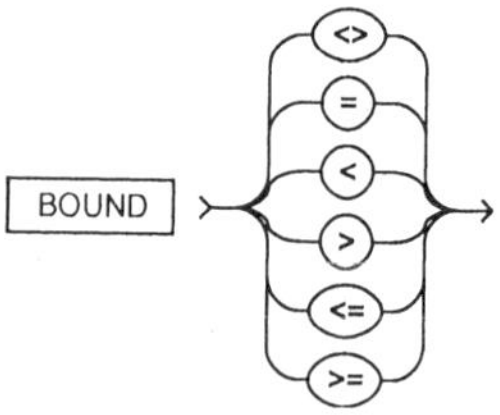

Figure 5-14. exMQL BOUND options

- `<ACTIONS> ::= /[ action || ',' ]/ ;`

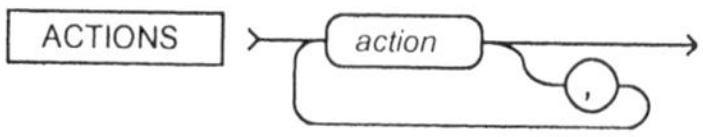

Figure 5-15. exMQL ACTIONS Clause

For this second function, and particularly selection and join conditions, each row in a query result set that is returned for an information request is checked against these conditions, and if the conditions are upheld then the query results remain intact. Otherwise, the affected rows are removed from the query results.

Multiple conditions are conjoined by the logical operators AND, or otherwise OR. As illustrated a selection condition is defined as a data item bound to a literal value, i.e. a string or numeric value. A join condition is the comparison of two data items, while a negotiation condition is a system-defined attribute that is bound to a literal value. The specification of conditions in a query is optional.

The DO command is used to specify the procedural actions of a query (See Chapter 4). An action can be associated with a particular condition, and accordingly will be executed if the condition is determined to be true. Also, an action can be associated with a query in general, and so will be executed on the successful match of a query. The specification of actions in a query is optional.

- `<DELETE_QUERY>    ::=    'DELETE'    query_name    -[ 'CASCADE' ]- ;`

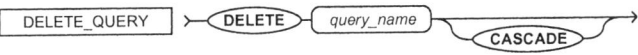

Figure 5-16. exMQL DELETE QUERY Clause

- `<DELETE_RULE> ::= 'DELETE' /[ rule_name || ',' ]/ 'IN' query_name ;`

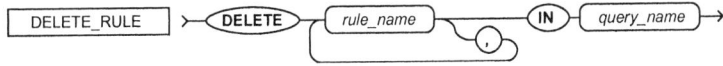

Figure 5-17. exMQL DELETE RULE Clause

- `<DELETE_CONDITION> ::= 'DELETE' /[ condition_name || ',' ]/ 'IN' query_name ;`

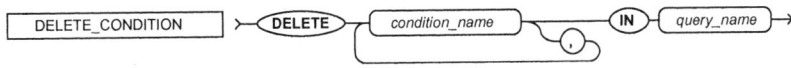

Figure 5-18. exMQL DELETE CONDITION Clause

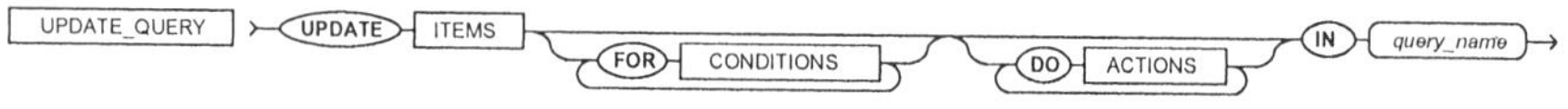

- ```
  <UPDATE_QUERY>    ::=   'UPDATE'   <ITEMS>   *['FOR'
  <CONDITIONS>]* *['DO' <ACTIONS>]* 'IN' query_name
  ;
  ```

Figure 5-19. exMQL UPDATE QUERY Clause

As illustrated in Figs. 5-16 – 5-19, a query can be removed from the Blackboard with the DELETE QUERY command. As noted in Section 2 all queries are unique to the system and so the DELETE command followed by the unique query identifier removes the query from the Blackboard. If the optional command CASCADE is specified then the all queries related to the particular proxy database server will be removed from the Blackboard.

If it is necessary to delete a rule, the DELETE RULE command is used. This rule takes two values as input, the rule name which is specified after the DELETE RULE command, and the query name which appears after the IN command. This command deletes all conditions associated with a query. More than one rule can be specified for deletion in each delete rule command.

The DELETE CONDITION command removes a condition from an existing rule, and can accommodate more than one condition specified as a comma-delimited list.

A query can be completely revised through the use of the UPDATE QUERY command. New data items and conditions included in the update query command will be added to the existing query, and existing items will be unchanged if they are specified as such in the query. If existing items are modified then these will be similarly modified in the rulebase. If existing items are not provided in the update query command, then these will be automatically removed from the existing query.

The above description of the exMQL has been provided for instructive purposes only, since in common usage these commands will be hidden from the user, as the exMQGS is regarded as the standard programmatic interface for the TSCM. Accordingly, each command represented in the above figures has a menu-driven counterpart in the exMGQS. Furthermore, our functional implementation of exMQL differs from the commands represented above as illustrated in Appendix A, but the definitions and procedures of all commands still remain intact.
  ```

Chapter 6

THE IMPLEMENTATION OF THE TWO-STAGE COLLABORATION MODEL

1. GLOBAL DATABASE QUERY IN A SUPPLY-CHAIN

This chapter illustrates how the elements of the TSCM interoperate to implement global query in a supply-chain. The illustration in Fig. 6-1, depicts the supply-chain for a typical enterprise, and also identifies additional suppliers and retailers that do not participate in the supply-chain of the enterprise.

The significant issue here is that suppliers may belong to multiple supply-chains, and perhaps are subject to various scheduling demands. The ability to determine demand forecasts would improve cycle time and optimize inventories, among other benefits, but in the traditional supply-chain this would be a difficult undertaking. The TSCM on the other hand, offers the opportunity to view shared data at all levels of the supply-chain, via the queries shared at the Blackboard, and the data available in the associated export databases. For example, the material inventory published by the SCD export database in Figure 6-2, should be visible throughout enterprise. Accordingly, the opportunity to access and manipulate a supplier's shared data, regardless of position in the supply-chain is realized in the TSCM.

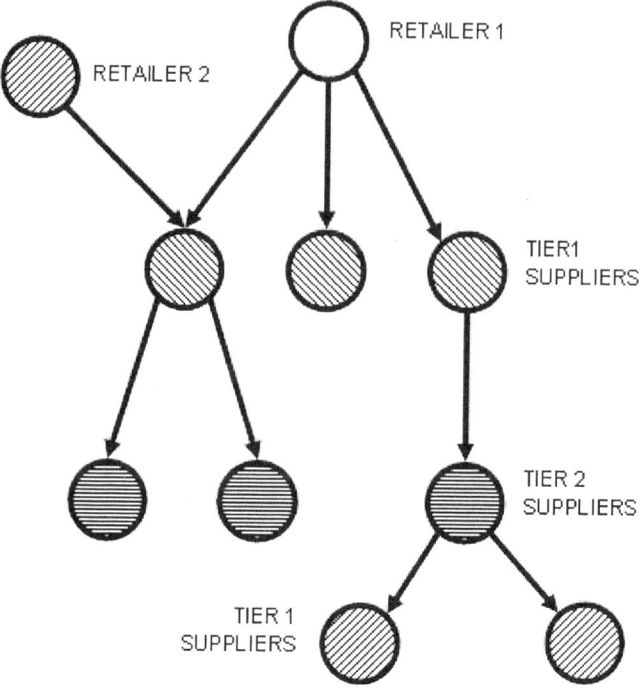

Figure 6-1. Traditional Supply-Chain

1.1   The Global Query Process: A Working Example

The illustrations that follow depict the various activities required for global query in the supply-chain. As expressed in the previous chapters and depicted in Fig. 6-3, the TSCM consists of interconnected export databases participating as publishers and/or subscribers, as well as the global Blackboard and global Metadatabase.

Each export database submits queries corresponding to the role in which it participates in the TSCM, that is, it submits a request (See ❶ in Fig. 6-3) (subscription query) if it is participating as a subscriber, and an offer (See ❷ in Fig. 6-3) (publication query), if participating as a publisher. When the Blackboard encounters a query it initiates the query matching process to identify queries in the query database that complement the supplied query.

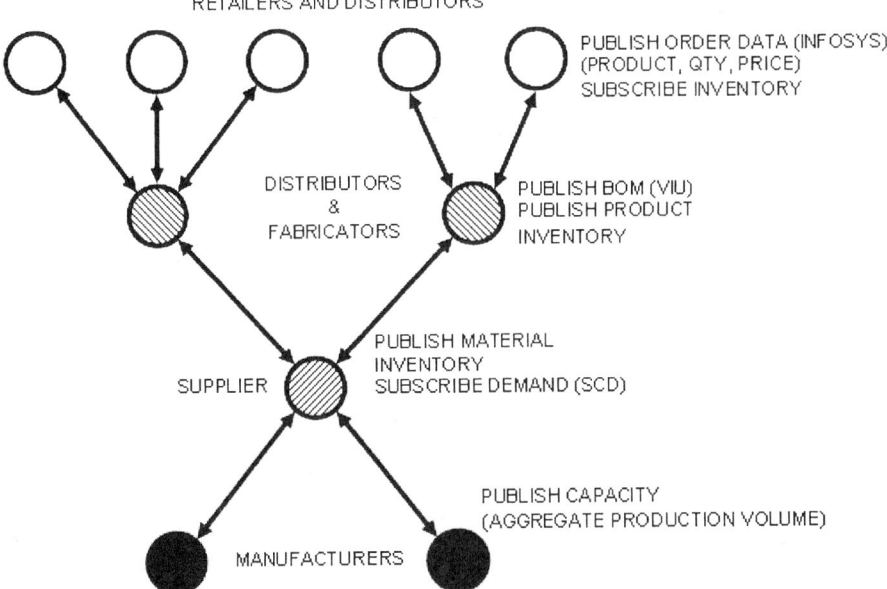

Figure 6-2. TSCM facilitated Supply-Chain

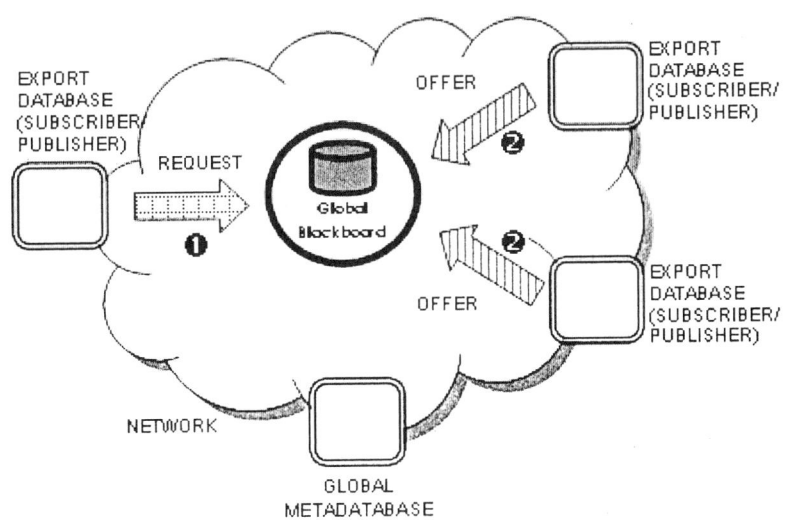

Figure 6-3. Global Query in a Supply-Chain

The queries sent between export databases and the Blackboard are described in an XML-based query language, exMQL which is illustrated in Chapter 5 and Appendix A. The information offer and information request corresponding to the queries in Fig. 6-3 are depicted in Table 6-1 and Table 6-2. Table 6-1 illustrates that a supplier has shared the production data for the product "paper", and specified an expiration date for the query. Table 6-2 on the other hand, illustrates an information request for a product with a part identifier "paper" and additional attributes to constrain the query. These are negotiation constraints that include the cost that is offered for the item, and the associated currency.

Table 6-1. Information Offer

```
<exMQL SYSTEMID="UUID_SYSTEM">
  <query command="put" ID="UUID_QUERY">
    <items>
      <item>PARTNAME</item>
      <item>PARTDESC</item>
      <item>NUM_COMPLETED</item>
    </items>
    <condlist>
      <cond type="SEL" loper="PARTNAME" op="eq" roper="PAPER"
      />
      <cond type="NEG" loper="EXPIRE" op="eq" roper="121304"
      />
    </condlist>
  </query>
</exMQL>
```

Table 6-2. Information Request

```
<exMQL SYSTEMID="UUID_SYSTEM">
  <query command="get" ID="UUID_QUERY">
    <items>
      <item>PARTNAME</item>
    </items>
    <condlist>
      <cond type="SEL" loper="PART_ID" op="eq" roper="PAPER"
      />
      <cond type="NEG" loper="PRICE" op="eq" roper="10.00" />
      <cond type="NEG" loper="LANG" op="eq" roper="EN" />
      <cond type="NEG" loper="CURRENCY" op="eq" roper="USD" />
    </condlist>
  </query>
</exMQL>
```

It is important to note that both information requests and offers are uniquely defined in each export database, and so are also uniquely defined in the global domain by appending the unique system identifier to each query. This is represented by the universally unique identifier (UUID) in the figures above. Furthermore, these examples use the more familiar data item names for illustrative purposes only in Table 6-1 and Table 6-2, which are viewable in the exMGQS. However the internal representation of these data items in the Metadatabase and the Blackboard that are declared in these messages utilizes a globally unique identifier, the ITEMCODE (See Appendix B) that would be substituted in the actual queries.

1.2   Query Matching and Allocation at the Blackboard

Fig. 6-4 illustrates the internal operations of the Blackboard when a query is encountered. When a new query is received at the Blackboard the Network Monitor detects and passes the query on to the Message Processor (See ❷ in Fig. 6-4), where it is validated and the query attributes extracted and then submitted (See ❸ in Fig. 6-4) to the Blackboard Database Management System (BDBMS) for processing. The Blackboard identifies matching queries via the execution of the *matching, combination matching* (optional) and *constraint matching* algorithms illustrated in Chapter 4. If necessary, the *Combination Matching* algorithm in Chapter 4 is executed to combine matching results from individual export databases in an attempt to identify a combination exact match. Accordingly, the global Metadatabase may be included in this query process (See ❹ in Fig. 6-4) to assess if the data items from the individual queries are directly connected in any fashion. Following a match in any form, the query is assigned (See ❺❻❼ in Fig. 6-4 and ❶ in Fig. 6-5.

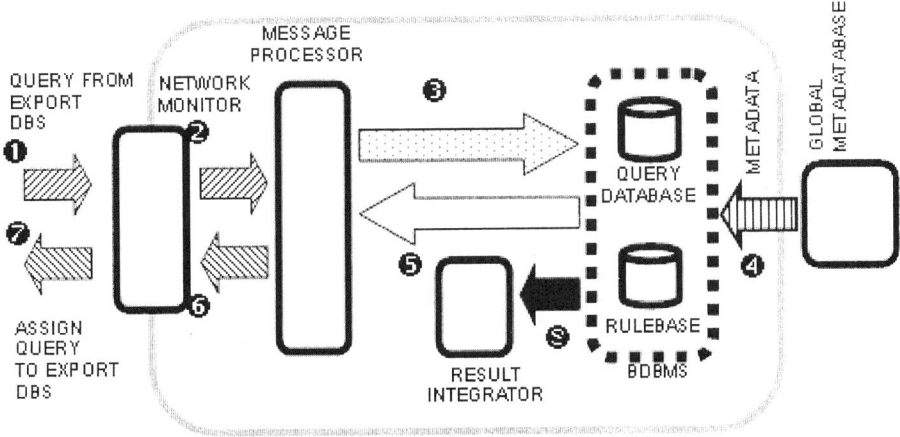

Figure 6-4. Internal Blackboard Query Processing

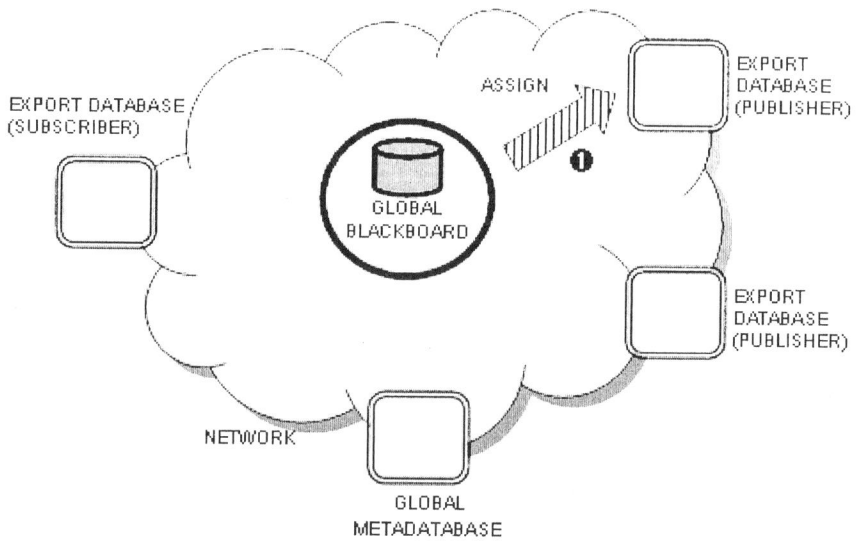

Figure 6-5. Allocation of Query to Export Database

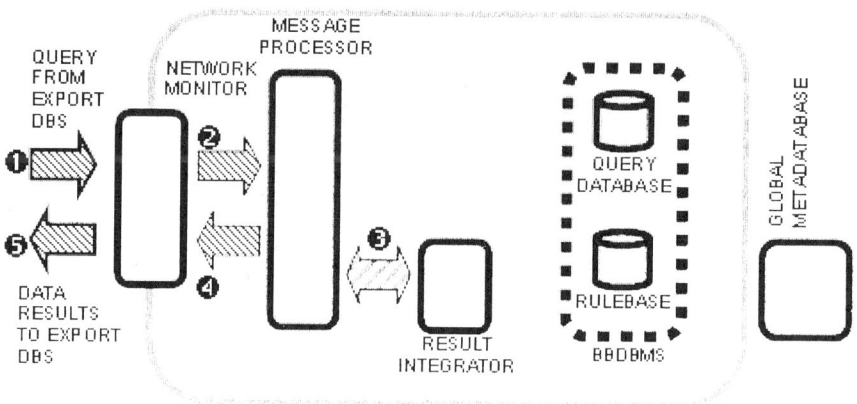

Figure 6-6. Internal Operations of Blackboard – Result Integration

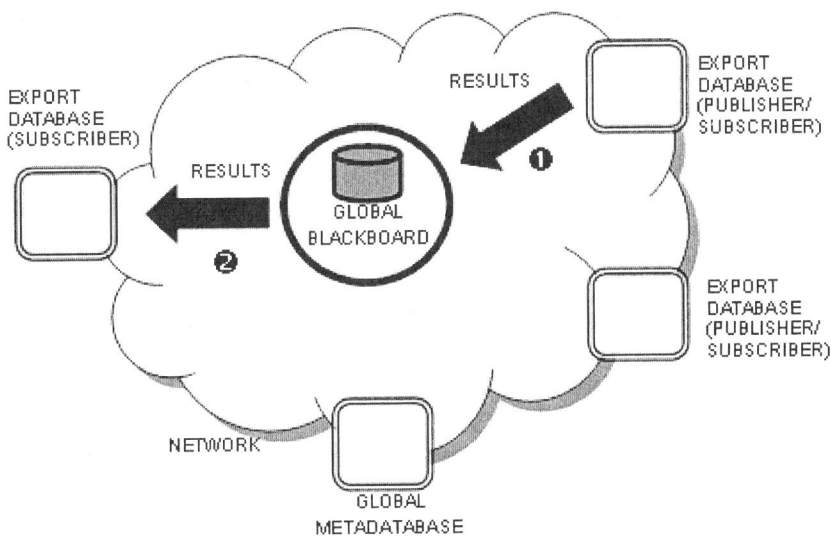

Figure 6-7. Results Processing

When the Blackboard encounters a combination match it issues query execution requests to the affected export databases (See ❺❻❼ in Fig. 6-4), and concurrently submits an integration script to the result integrator (See ❽ in Fig. 6-4). Each execution request contains the data items required from the affected export databases, and a reference to the affected query. The integration script is registered with the Network Monitor, such that when the query results are returned to the Blackboard, it is routed to the result integrator for processing. When all results have been returned to the Blackboard from the individual export databases, the results are integrated (See ❶❷❸❹❺ in Fig. 6-6) and then forwarded to the requestor (See ❶❷ in Fig. 6-7.

The discussion of query execution is postponed until Section 1.4, so that the process of how to add a query to the Blackboard in the event query matching fails can be discussed, in Section 1.3.

1.2.1   Encountering a Match that Requires External Input

There are various instances that will require the Blackboard to seek external input. In the event the Blackboard encounters a data feasible solution, but cannot determine a constraint feasible solution, then the Blackboard issues a notification of the conflict. The working example (See Table 6-1 and Table 6-2) depicts a subset match, and data feasible solution from the perspective of the information request; however, it is constraint infeasible as defined by the constraint matching algorithm (See Chapter 4) due to the non-matching constraints specified in each query. The information request contains selection conditions and negotiation conditions, whereas the information offer contains only selection conditions that do not match each other. In light of this conflict, if it is not possible for the Blackboard to determine a result, the affected parties, i.e. the subscriber and publisher would be notified of the conflict, and would be prompted to modify the relevant queries.

1.3   Insert Query Operation on the Blackboard

In the event a match is not found, the query is added to the Blackboard for subsequent processing at a later time. The Message Processor (See ❷ in Fig. 6-4) also transforms the supplied query into its SQL equivalent, which is then submitted to the Blackboard upon the failure to identify a match. The SQL statements are arranged in a particular order to preserve dependency constraints that exists in the query database and rulebase. It is necessary therefore to create a mapping from the query message representation into a relational format, to satisfy these dependency issues. As illustrated in Fig. 6-8, the query message can be realized as a directed graph (Florescu and Kossmann 1999; Liu and Vincent 2003), where the message is the root of the tree. The tree consists of nodes that correspond to the various internal elements of the query message, while the leaves of the tree correspond to either attributes of a node or a text node. The attributes and leaves are represented as shaded circles, and the nodes as hollow circles. The diagram illustrates where the various message elements are stored in the Blackboard. The exMQL element identifies the origin of the message, and so contains a SYSTEM identifier attribute which is stored in the SYSTEM entity, while the query element additionally contains a unique QUERY identifier, which is stored in the QUERY entity. The same goes for data items referenced by the ITEM entity, which also must create corresponding relationships in the adjacent MAPPED_TO and DESCRIBES tables (See Fig. 5-2 and Appendix B) for a description of these meta-entities, meta-relationships and their attributes.

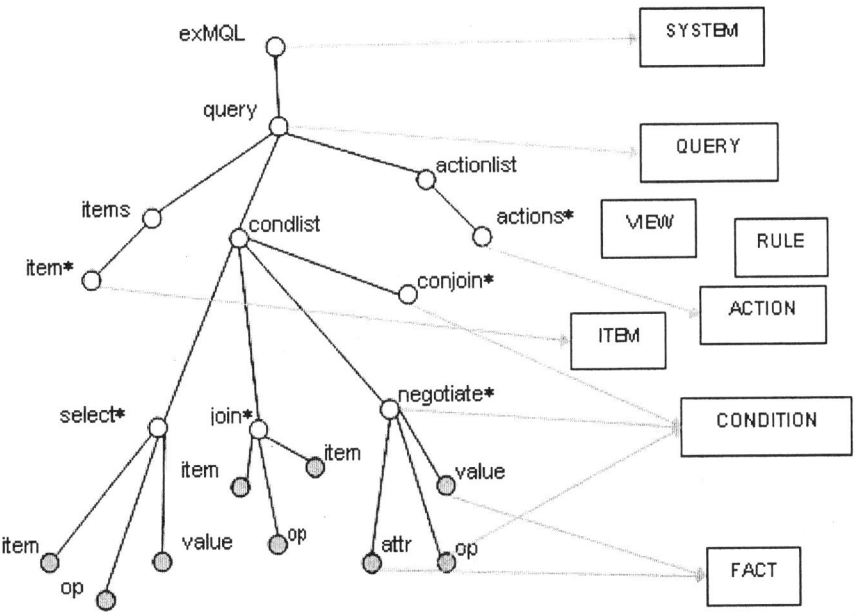

Figure 6-8. Mapping Query Schema to Blackboard Schema

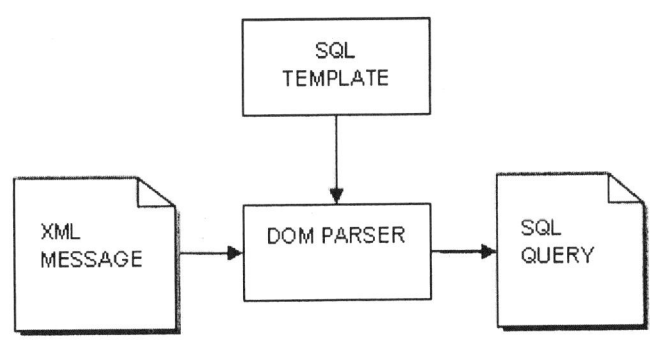

Figure 6-9. Query Message Transformation to SQL

A DOM (Document Object Model) Parser is used to transform the XML message to its equivalent SQL query format. As depicted in Fig. 6-9, the DOM Parser is the link between the XML message and the SQL query, however a corresponding template that describes the resulting format of the SQL query is also required as input to the DOM Parser. The template addresses the dependency constraints that were raised above.

Table 6-3. Commands for Information Offer illustrated in Table 6-1

```
SYSTEM (SYSNAME) VALUES ('UUID_SYSTEM');
QUERY (QNAME, SYSNAME, QTYPE, TIMESTAMP)
VALUES ('UUID_QUERY','UUID_SYSTEM','OFFER',20041213000000);
VIEW (VNAME) VALUES ('UUID_QUERY_VIEW_1');
ITEM (ITEMCODE, ITEMNAME, SYSNAME)
VALUES ('UUID_SYSTEM_ITEMCODE_1','PARTNAME', 'UUID_SYSTEM');
ITEM (ITEMCODE, ITEMNAME, SYSNAME)
VALUES ('UUID_SYSTEM_ITEMCODE_2','PARTDESC', 'UUID_SYSTEM');
ITEM (ITEMCODE, ITEMNAME, SYSNAME)
VALUES ('UUID_SYSTEM_ITEMCODE_2','NUM_COMPLETED',
'UUID_SYSTEM');
DESCRIBES (QNAME, ITEMCODE)
VALUES ('UUID_QUERY', 'PARTNAME');
DESCRIBES (QNAME, ITEMCODE)
VALUES ('UUID_QUERY', 'PARTDESC');
DESCRIBES (QNAME, ITEMCODE)
VALUES ('UUID_QUERY', 'NUM_COMPLETED');
FACT (FACTID, FACTNAME, FACTYPE, FACTVALUE, VALUEOF)
VALUES ('FACTID_1', '', 1, '', 'UUID_SYSTEM_ITEMCODE_1') ;
FACT (FACTID, FACTNAME, FACTYPE, FACTVALUE, VALUEOF)
VALUES ('FACTID_2', '', 0, 'SHELL', '') ;
CONDITION (CONDID, LOPER, OPERATOR, ROPER)
VALUES ('CONDID_1', 'FACTID_1', 'eq', 'FACTID_2) ;
RULE (CONDID) VALUES ('CONDID_1') ;
FACT (FACTID, FACTNAME, FACTYPE, FACTVALUE, VALUEOF)
VALUES ('PARTIDeqSHELL', 4, '', 'CONDID_1') ;
```

The resulting output of this transformation algorithm for the information offer depicted in Table 6-1 is illustrated in Table 6-3 above. The INSERT statements have been truncated, i.e. the prefix "INSERT INTO" has been removed from each statement to improve readability.

1.4   Query Execution at the Export Database

Figure 6-10 illustrates the internal operations of the export database when a query execution request has been encountered. The Network Monitor detects the query execution request issued by the Blackboard and redirects (See ❷ in Fig. 6-10) it to the Message Processor that transforms the query into a SQL SELECT statement. The query is then redirected (See ❸ in Fig. 6-10) to the export database system for processing. Query transformation is accomplished in a similar manner to that described in Section 1.3. The results are then sent to the Blackboard (See ❹❺❻ in Fig. 6-10).

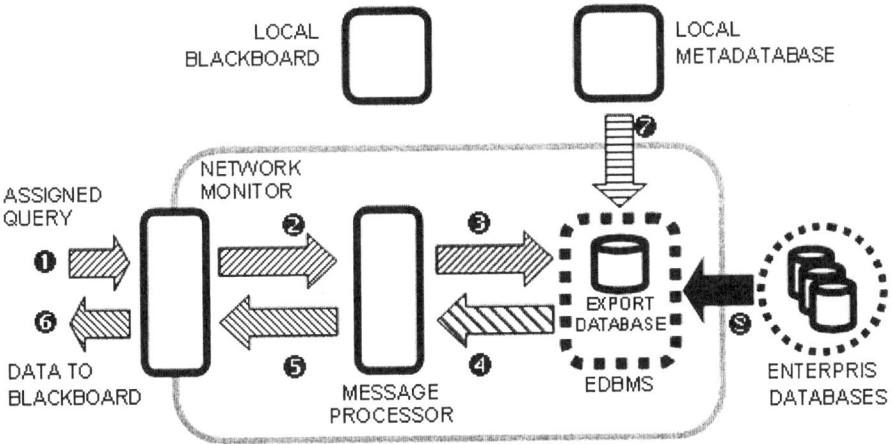

Figure 6-10. Internal Operations of the Export Database

The enterprise databases are the source of data for the export databases. When the publication query is defined, this creates a corresponding schema in the export database, and the database is populated with the associated data from the enterprise databases (See ❽ in Fig. 6-10). At the same time, the local Metadatabase transforms the data values from the local attributes and values to their equivalent global attributes and values (See ❼ in Fig. 6-10).

2. THE PROTOTYPE OF THE TWO-STAGE COLLABORATION MODEL

2.1 Specifications of the Prototype Environment

The prototype considers the implementation of the Blackboard, Metadatabase and the attendant algorithms. The prototype development environment utilized the Fedora Linux Core 2 operating system, which was installed on a custom-built database and web server. The hardware and additional software utilized on the server had the following specifications:

- Dual Processor, Pentium 3 CPU, 900 MHz
- 1 GB Ram
- 2 x 80 GB Hard Drive, RAID 0
- PostgreSQL ORDBMS Version 7.4.7
- Apache Httpd Server, Version 2.0.51

- PHP Version 4.3.10

    The default installation options for all software utilized in the prototype were utilized, with the exception of PostgreSQL, which had to be modified to accept connections from the Apache web server. The additional steps that were required to configure the prototype environment are discussed in the following sub-section. A discussion about the operation of the exMGQS is also the subject of a subsequent sub-section.

2.2   Implementation of the Metadatabase and Blackboard

    Two PostgreSQL database schemas were created within a single database: *mdb* and *bb*, to contain the Metadatabase and Blackboard schemas respectively (See Appendix B for the Blackboard and Metadatabase Schema). The PostgreSQL ORDBMS maintains an additional definition for the term schema, as defined in the PostgreSQL 7.4 manual:

> "A schema is essentially a namespace: it contains named objects (tables, data types, functions, and operators) whose names may duplicate those of other objects existing in other schemas. Named objects are accessed either by "qualifying" their names with the schema name as a prefix, or by setting a search path that includes the desired schema(s) (The PostgreSQL Global Development Group 2005)."

    This provided for a seamless integration of the Metadatabase and the Blackboard. Therefore, it was not necessary to consider the overhead required to communicate between disparate databases when using an external message protocol, as well as the issues of dealing with multiple database connections if different databases were used. The schema facility allows both structures to be contained within one database, and the internal operations inclusive of the algorithms in Chapter 4, and exMQL are confined to this single database.

    The algorithms in Chapter 4 were implemented in PL/pgSQL the procedural programming language for the PostgreSQL Database System, and installed into the database server.

2.3 Query Formulation using the exMGQS

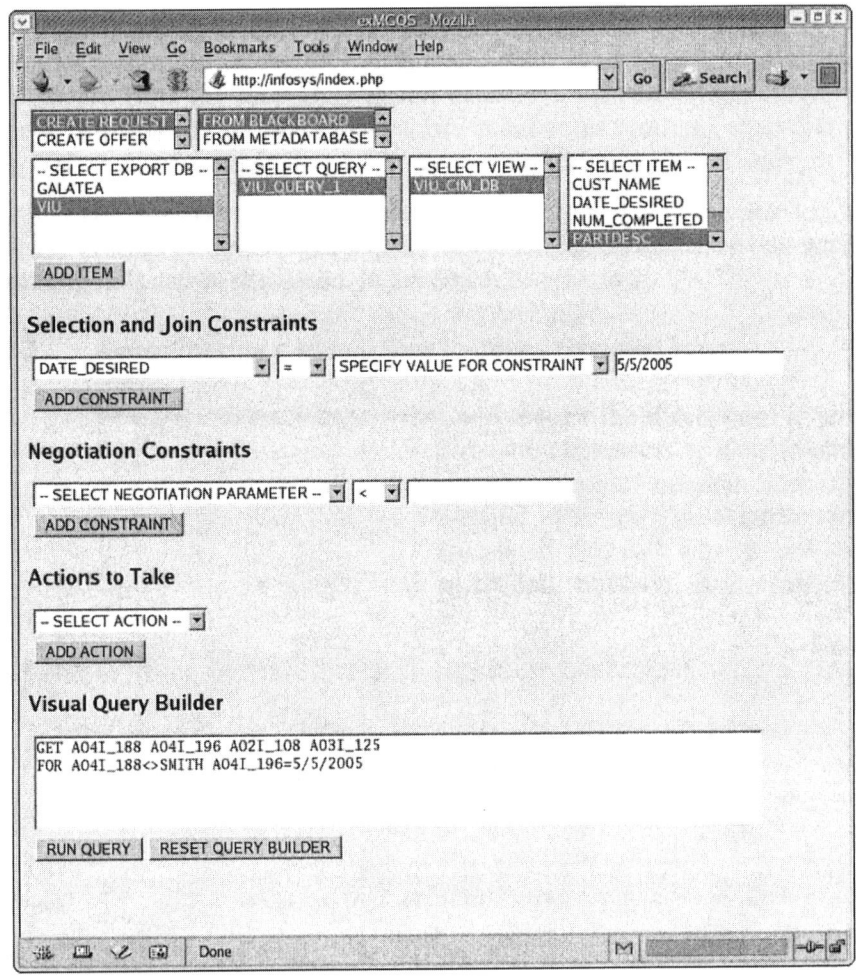

Figure 6-11. Extended Metadatabase Global Query System Graphical User Interface

The exMGQS application by default resides at the global site. In the event that an export database is masquerading as a global Blackboard in a peer-to-peer match session, then the exMGQS will be installed on that particular system as well. Both subscription and publication queries are constructed via the GUI of the exMGQS, an example of which is illustrated in Fig. 6-11. The GUI is implemented as a JavaScript front-end, with embedded PHP functionality to connect to the Metadatabase and Blackboard, however all TSCM functionality is isolated to the database system. The formulation of a subscription or publication query begins with the selection of the corresponding command in the list of tasks, that is, CREATE REQUEST and CREATE OFFER respectively. This activates the list of data sources, which include the Blackboard and Metadatabase. The selection of a data source activates the display of resources available for the combination of previously selected options, which is described in Table 6-4.

Therefore, the selection of the task and data source reveals an adjacent list of options listing the resources indicated in Table 6-4. Consequently, selecting an export database, when creating a request, reveals an adjacent list of options describing the queries published by the selected export database. Choosing a query from the list of queries reveals an adjacent list of options describing the views contained in the selected query. Finally, the selection of a view, from the list of views, reveals an adjacent list of data items that are contained in the view, and recursively the publication query issued by the selected export database. This procedure is identical for all the combinations listed in Table 6-4, and can be repeated until the information content of the query is satisfied. However, in combinations 1, 2 and 3 in Table 6-4, the data items selected may span multiple export databases when selecting data items from the Blackboard, and may span multiple applications when selecting data items from the Metadatabase (See Chapter 4). Combination 4 on the other hand is limited to the local data model only, that is, the data items can only span the applications contained within this data model.

Table 6-4. Resources Displayed in exMGQS given Selected Task and Data Source

Combination	Task	Data Source	exMGQS Display
1	Create Request	From Blackboard	All Export Databases (Publication Queries Only)
2	Create Request	From Metadatabase	Global Metadata Model
3	Create Offer	From Blackboard	All Export Databases (Subscription Queries Only)
4	Create Offer	From Metadatabase	Local Metadata Model Only

The Visual Query Builder provides a snapshot of the current state of the query as each data item is selected for inclusion in the query.

Once all data items have been selected for inclusion in the query, then constraints on these data items can be specified, if required. The data items previously selected are all candidates for attributes in the selection and join constraints, and so are made available for qualification by the exMGQS. The participant qualifies data items by specifying parameters (or data items in the case of join conditions) for the attributes, and also selecting a relational operator to compare both quantities. Negotiation constraints can also be specified to further qualify the query; however the attributes that constitute these constraints are not derived from data items and do not exist in any particular system meta-model, but rather are globally-defined at run-time. Finally, the participant can specify *actions* to take given specific outcomes of a match session at the Blackboard (See Chapter 4). These actions are also globally defined at run-time.

The query formulation is then complete when the participant submits the query to the Global Blackboard. In summary, the query formulation process encompasses the following procedure, which is derived from the query formulation algorithm found in Cheung (Cheung and Hsu 1996), Page 75:

Table 6-5. Query Formulation Algorithm

Repeat (for each visit)
Step 1 – Traverse to the data item identified at the ith visit and select the data item to be included in the query
Step 2 – Specify the selection conditions C^{SC} and join conditions C^J that will be imposed on the selected data items
Until no more intended data items are specified
Step 3 – Specify the negotiation conditions C^N, and actions A that will be imposed on the query.

The exMGQS simplifies query formulation due to the interactive process of adding data items and constraints to the visual query builder, which therefore reduces lexical, structural and syntactical errors that are typical in command-line query formulation. It is still however necessary to parse the query in order to validate the syntax, and also the semantics of the query. In this regard, emphasis is placed on the constraints to verify that the format and domain of the parameters are consistent with the data items (specifically, selection constraints) to which there are applied. Furthermore, the exMQGS ensure that the data items in join constraints are consistent with each other.

Chapter 7

THE JUSTIFICATION OF THE TWO-STAGE COLLABORATION MODEL

1. OVERVIEW

The TSCM differs at a fundamental level from traditional global query methods and the various other approaches for information matching, primarily in the contribution of the publication methods, and the Blackboard Match Engine. The realization of the database platform as its enabling technology establishes the TSCM, as a significant contribution to the global query field.

Traditional global database query, as realized in federated database systems offer greater "depth" to information exchange, relative to current information exchange technologies; however the technology has not embraced these virtual enterprises and so are limited by their traditional architectures. Conversely, private and industrial information exchanges facilitate information exchange within the supply-chain; however the "depth" of collaboration is limited to document and message exchange. Databases are integral to such collaboration infrastructures, however they are typically ancillary elements of the integration, and support the construction/population of said collaboration documents. In a different approach, software agents in Multi-Agent Systems are endowed with intelligence to make complex decisions, however the implementation of these agents and the underlying multi-agent infrastructure is no easy task. Current results in the field depend on heuristics to define the match methods and agent capabilities. These characteristics however can differ across the various multi-agent architectures thus preventing interoperability and requiring custom solutions to facilitate integration.

In this chapter the TSCM is justified through a comparison with similar results in the field, and peripheral research domains. This analysis emphasizes the qualitative aspects of these related contributions, and presents a discussion of the advantages/disadvantages of the TSCM with respect to these results. But first, the performance of the TSCM is assessed, specifically focusing on the Blackboard Match Engine and its attendant matching algorithms. By using relational algebra, acceptable query trees are determined, which allow for the identification of query plans, such that the performance of the algorithms can be evaluated. This quantitative analysis emphasizes the worst-case performance. Section 2 presents the discussion of this quantitative analysis, while Section 3 and onwards presents the qualitative analysis previously mentioned.

2.   A PERFORMANCE ASSESSMENT OF THE TSCM

As the TSCM is implemented as a procedural language module of a relational database, its performance is intrinsically tied to the capabilities of the database software and underlying hardware. For this research the PostgreSQL Object-Relational Database Management System (ORDBMS) was used, which is installed on the operating system hardware and software described in Chapter 6. An execution plan is readily determined in PostgreSQL; however, given the lack of realistic data, a generic analysis of the matching algorithms is performed to assess the performance limitations of the Blackboard. Since the database system will determine the execution plan, which then may vary by database platform, in this analysis the worst-case execution plan/performance, or highest cost estimate, of the matching algorithms is derived. The cost estimate quantity correlates to the algorithm with the most number of pages/blocks transferred from disk during a database query, which is a popular measure of database performance. The analysis however excludes other relevant query costs that do heavily influence the cost estimate, because (1) these are difficult-to-acquire measures of performance, and (2) the values are specific to the hardware, software, and communication platforms in which the database participates. These additional costs include computational, communication, and storage costs. Since the algorithms are implemented on the *centralized* Blackboard database system, then the *communication costs* between the export databases and the Blackboard can be ignored. *Computational costs* can also be ignored since this determines the cost of performing operations in memory, which would be difficult to assess. Moreover, *storage cost* is similarly excluded since these consider the storage of intermediate query results during the execution of a query plan. The *access cost of secondary storage* i.e. the disk access read and write times, provides the only relevant measure of performance that is widely accepted, but the analysis only considers the disk read times.

Table 7-1. SQL Query Corresponding to Algorithm 1

```
SELECT D.QNAME, COUNT(D.ITEMCODE)
FROM describes AS D, query AS Q
WHERE ITEMCODE
IN (itemcode_list)
AND D.QNAME = Q.QNAME
AND Q.TYPE ≠ query_type
GROUP BY D.QNAME;
```

Table 7-1 depicts an SQL query that corresponds to the *matching algorithm* illustrated in Chapter 4. This can be converted to a relational algebra expression to assist in the evaluation of the query execution plan. The expression in Eq. (1) depicts an acceptable query plan for the algorithm, in that it moves the select operation to the bottom of the query tree, uses equi-joins to join tables, and projects necessary attributes when possible. The size of the QUERY table (Q), and the DESCRIBES table (D) are restricted by applying the selection conditions, thus reducing the size of the relations participating in joins. Note also that a non-standard symbol G is employed to describe the GROUP BY clause – the prefix indicates the attribute the query should be grouped on, whereas the suffix indicates the aggregate functions applied to the adjacent attribute.

$$\pi_{\substack{qname,\\itemcount}} \left(\begin{array}{l} \pi_{qname}\left(\sigma_{type \neq \text{QUERY\_TYPE}}(Q)\right) \\[2ex] \infty_{Q.qname = D.qname} \\[2ex] {}_{qname}\mathsf{G}_{COUNT\ itemcode}\left(\pi_{\substack{qname,\\itemcode}}\left(\sigma_{itemcode \in \text{ITEMCODE\_LIST}}(D)\right)\right) \end{array} \right) \quad (1)$$

To begin the analysis a number of assumptions are made. As illustrated in Table 7-2, the QUERY table has a tuple size of 118 bytes, determined from Appendix B by assuming fixed width fields (i.e CHAR) as opposed to variable width fields (i.e. VARCHAR). Moreover, this discussion considers only the essential attributes in the QUERY table, which includes {QNAME, QTYPE, TIMESTAMP} required for query matching.

Summing the fixed widths of these fields totals 118 bytes, where QNAME constitutes 100 bytes, QTYPE, 10 bytes, and the TIMESTAMP is a fixed date/time field of 8 bytes. We will ignore tuple headers (metadata) in this analysis. The analysis is repeated for the DESCRIBES table to identify a tuple width of 200 bytes, which considers the QNAME and ITEMCODE attributes only. Furthermore, since the number of records is unknown for the QUERY and DESCRIBES table, then $|Q|$ and $|D|$ are declared as these variables. Finally, an assessment of the cost of basic operations, or the disk access times, will require an understanding of the basic units of storage on the disks. For this reason, the PostgreSQL page/block size of 8192 bytes is used as an estimate of the unit of storage, noting that this value is adjustable in PostgreSQL, and will likely also differ by database vendor. These quantities are summarized in Table 7-2.

Table 7-2. Statistical and Assumed Variables for Blackboard Database

Feature	Value
Cardinality, Q	$|Q|$
Cardinality, D	$|D|$
Page Size/Block Size	8192 bytes
Tuple Size, Q	118 bytes
Tuple Size, D	200 bytes

With the data provided in Table 7-2, it is now possible to determine the number of pages/blocks that the QUERY and DESCRIBES consume on the disk, and so determine the number of disk accesses required in the initial operations on the respective database tables. The blocking factor (*bfr*) defines the number of records that are contained in a block, and so it is possible to determine the number of blocks required for each table, which is a function of the number of tuples in a table. Accordingly,

$$bfr_Q = \lfloor 8192/118 \rfloor \Rightarrow b_Q = \lceil |Q|/bfr_Q \rceil = \lceil |Q|/69 \rceil \tag{2}$$

$$bfr_D = \lfloor 8192/200 \rfloor \Rightarrow b_D = \lceil |D|/bfr_D \rceil = \lceil |D|/40 \rceil \tag{3}$$

Given this information, then it is now possible to determine the cost estimates for the matching algorithm. To simplify the analysis, the query is deconstructed and the cost estimates of the individual operations are determined. The analysis begins with the *project* and *select* operation on the QUERY table as depicted in Eq. (4).

$$Op_1 = \pi_{qname}\left(\sigma_{type \neq \text{QUERY\_TYPE}}(Q)\right) \tag{4}$$

Since TYPE is a non-key attribute of Q, then it is necessary to perform a full-table scan on Q to determine the tuples that match TYPE $\neq$ QUERY_TYPE. With the assumption of a uniform distribution, the approximate number of results returned is $|Q|/2$ since the attribute TYPE considers two distinct values, and so roughly half of the tuples will match QUERY_TYPE. The estimate of the number of tuples returned from operation 1, denoted r_1, is depicted in Eq. (5). But, the performance is determined by the number of page reads, and so the corresponding cost estimate for this selection condition C_1, which assumes that half the pages have to be read before the results are found is depicted in Eq. (6). Note however that the *project* operator reduces the number of attributes in the result set, and so the *blocking factor* used corresponds to the size of this intermediate result, r_1 set and not $|Q|$ that was specified above.

$$r_1 = |Q| - \frac{|Q|}{2} = \frac{|Q|}{2} \tag{5}$$

$$C_1 = \frac{b_1}{2} = \frac{r_1/bfr_1}{2} = \frac{25 * |Q|}{8192} \tag{6}$$

The next operation in Eq. (7) is split into two distinct parts, (1) the *select* and *project* of QNAME and ITEMCODE, and (2) the grouping by attribute QNAME. The *select* operation can be transformed to a disjunctive condition, consisting of equality conditions on the ITEMCODE attribute, which are connected by the OR logical operator. It will be necessary to perform a full-scan on the table, because of the composite key <QNAME, ITEMCODE> and the fact that the *select* operator is on the ITEMCODE attribute only.

$$Op_2 = {}_{qname}\mathfrak{I}_{COUNT\ itemcode}\left(\pi_{qname,\ itemcode}\left(\sigma_{itemcode \in \text{ITEMCODE\_LIST}}(D)\right)\right) \tag{7}$$

The estimate of the number of tuples returned from this operation, r_{2a} is depicted in Eq. (8) (Silberschatz, Korth et al. 2002), where m is the number of ITEMCODE attributes in the selection condition, and s_i is the selection cardinality of the ith attribute given the associated equality constraint. Estimating s_i does present a challenge, since each query, and accordingly the data items it contains is independent from other queries. As a result, an assumption of a uniform distribution in i is probably not a reasonable one to make. In this regard, database statistics would provide for a more accurate estimate, and would be the proper approach to take. However, since such statistics are unavailable, a uniform distribution in i is assumed (subsequent analysis will test the effect that additional distribution models, e.g. Ziphian Distribution, will have on these estimates). Given this assumption of a uniform distribution, all values of i are equally likely to be in D, and therefore $s_i = |D|/m$ and r_{2a} is transformed to r_{2b}. The *project* operation terminates the first part of operation 2, which does not modify the tuple size; consequently the corresponding number of blocks required by this intermediate relation remains the same.

$$r_{2a} = |D| * \left[1 - \left(1 - \frac{s_i}{|D|} \right) * \left(1 - \frac{s_{i+1}}{|D|} \right) * \ldots * \left(1 - \frac{s_m}{|D|} \right) \right] \tag{8}$$

$$r_{2b} = |D| * \left[1 - \left(1 - \frac{1}{m} \right)^m \right] \tag{9}$$

The second part of Operation 2 in Eq. (7) is more complex than the first, involving sorting and grouping of the results by the QNAME attribute and then computing the COUNT aggregate function. As recommended in (Garcia-Molina, Ullman et al. 2002), the results from a grouping operation can range from one group to the number of distinct tuples in r_{2b}. However, since the grouping is performed on QNAME, the aforementioned assumption of uniformity can also be applied here, and so the number of tuples returned from operation 2 is estimated to be $r_{2b}/2$, on average. Equation (10) illustrates the complete result. The corresponding cost of this result set is illustrated in Eq. (11).

$$r_2 = \frac{|D|}{2} * \left[1 - \left(1 - \frac{1}{m} \right)^m \right] \tag{10}$$

$$C_2 = \left(\frac{|D|}{2} * \left[1 - \left(1 - \frac{1}{m} \right)^m \right] \right) \Big/ bfr_D \qquad (11)$$

The third operation considers the join of r_1 and r_2 (See Eq. (12)). Multiple join algorithms can be employed to evaluate this operation, e.g. nested-loop, sort-merge and the hash-join algorithm, among others. The nested-loop join algorithm is selected first to determine the result of operation 3.

$$Op_3 = Op_1 \bowtie_{Q.qname=D.qname} Op_2 \qquad (12)$$

The nested-loop join algorithm gives better performance when the table with the lower number of tuples is used as the outer-loop relation in the join. It is difficult to assess which quantity, r_1 or r_2 could be used as the outer relation, since r_1 considers one type of query, and r_2 considers both, and conversely, r_2 has a reduced set because of the grouping operation and r_1 does not. Therefore, the final analysis will demonstrate both results, and the effect it has on the cost estimate. The corresponding number of tuples resulting from a nested-loop join algorithm is depicted in Eq. (13). This result considers r_2 as the outer-relation in the join.

$$r_3 = r_2 + r_2 * r_1 \qquad (13)$$

Again, the number of page reads is the more interesting value, and so the corresponding cost of this operation can be determined with the formula depicted in Eq. (14) (Elmasri and Navathe 2000). Recall that this quantity excludes page writes, i.e. the writing of the result set to disk.

$$C_3 = b_2 + \left(b_2 * b_1 \right) \qquad (14)$$

To keep the unknowns in the cost estimate consistent, C_3 is transformed to C_{3a} as illustrated in Eq. (15). The last *project* operation does not alter the cost C_{3a}, and consequently this quantity remains unchanged.

$$C_{3a} = \frac{r_2}{bfr_2} + \left(\frac{r_2}{bfr_2} * \frac{r_1}{bfr_1} \right) \qquad (15)$$

With the results sizes, r_1 and r_2, and the quantities from Table 7-2 it is now possible to evaluate the performance of the matching algorithm. The evaluation considers the performance per table size, i.e. the cost estimate given the number of tuples in the Blackboard, given an average number of data items per attribute.

Lemma 1:   The number of tuples in DESCRIBES is directly proportional to the number of tuples in QUERY.

Proof: This is established by the foreign key relationship that DESCRIBES (D) has with QUERY (Q) on the attribute QNAME. Each query, when stored in D, requires at least n tuples, where n corresponds to the average number of data item in a query. Each of these data items references the particular query to which it belongs. Therefore given $|Q|$ queries, then the number of tuples in D is $n|Q|$. $n|Q|$ is substituted wherever the size of D is required, since D is a function of the number of tuples in Q. ∎

Therefore, the cost estimate for the query in Table 7-1 is the sum of the individual costs determined in Eq. (6), Eq. 11 and Eq. 14. Accordingly, Fig. 7-1 illustrates a plot of this cost as function of the number of queries that are in the Blackboard; given that on average there are five (5) data items per query.

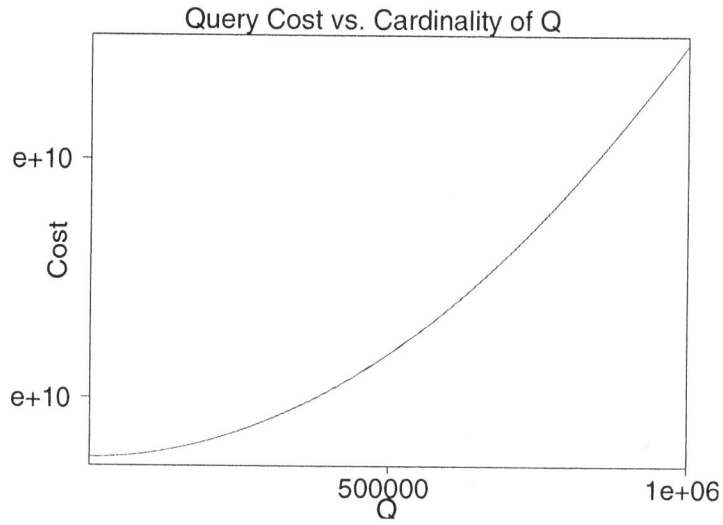

Figure 7-1. Query Cost vs. Cardinality of Q (Outer Relation – r_2)

Figure 7-2 is obtained by choosing r_1 as the outer relation in the nested-loop join algorithm. The plot indicates that there is an increase in the cost when choosing r_1 as the outer relation.

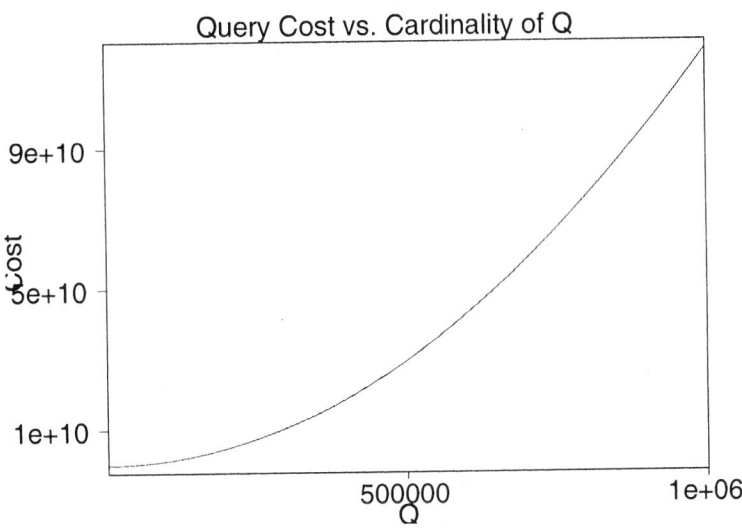

Figure 7-2. Query Cost vs. Cardinality of Q (Outer Relation – r_1)

Theorem: The complexity of the matching algorithm for a uniform set of offers and requests is no greater than $O(n^2)$, where n is the number of queries in the Blackboard.

Proof: The corresponding cost is determined by assuming that a, b, c, d are constants, and k is the number of tuples in the QUERY table. Since the queries and ITEMCODEs are assumed uniformly distributed, m is therefore a constant. From Lemma 1, the number of tuples in D is declared a function of the number of tuples in Q, therefore each instance of $|D|$ is replaced with $n|Q|$. The blocking factors are a constant, while the number of blocks consumed by each table is a function of the table size, and the blocking factor. Therefore, the sum of the cost estimates can be reduced to the following generic polynomial:

$$C = ak + bk + ck + dk^2 \Rightarrow C = (a+b+c)k + dk^2 \qquad (16)$$

Therefore, assuming a uniform distribution of the query table, the complexity of the matching algorithm is no greater than $O(n^2)$. ∎

The results here however do represent an overestimation of the performance of the matching algorithm. A database will choose the best execution plan it can, but this occurs only if the data structures are defined to support this selection. In the following section, certain adjustments are recommended to the logical model, which will force the implementation of better performing algorithms in the aforementioned operations, therefore providing for lower cost estimates and improved performance of the matching algorithm.

2.1 Adjusting the Logical Model to Improve TSCM Performance

The biggest contributor to the cost of the matching algorithm is the nested-loop join algorithm, and so adjustments to improve the matching performance are made here first. The alternative sort-merge algorithm will introduce a cost: $C = b_2 + b_1$, essentially a cost having linear complexity $O(n)$, but this requires that the corresponding input tuples, r_1 and r_2 are sorted on the join attribute QNAME, which currently is not guaranteed. The sorting in the sort-merge join operation increases the associated cost as indicated in Eq. (17) (Elmasri and Navathe 2000). This arises from the fact that the sort-merge algorithm must make multiple passes on r_1 and r_2; first to sort then to merge. Moreover, the estimate includes the cost to write the results back to disk.

$$C = (2 * b_2 * (1 + \log_2 b_2)) + (2 * b_1 * (1 + \log_2 b_1)) + b_2 + b_1 \qquad (17)$$

By choosing this adjustment, the performance complexity of the matching algorithm then becomes at most $O(n \log n)$.

As indicated above, the sort-merge has linear complexity if both r_1 and r_2 are already sorted. The QUERY table already contains an index on QNAME, but the WHERE clause in the select operation specifies the QTYPE attribute, which does not have an index. Therefore, a sorted result is not guaranteed. Creating a secondary index on this attribute will improve the select operation, such that $C_1 = x + s$, where s is the selection cardinality matching ¬QTYPE, and x is the number of levels in the secondary index. A B+-tree search tree used for the secondary index allows for this linear complexity, $O(n)$.

The DESCRIBES table contains an index on <QNAME, ITEMCODE>, but the IN clause in the select operation leads to the disjunctive condition previously mentioned, which requires the union of the results from the individual conditions. A secondary index could also be applied to ITEMCODE, resulting in the similar cost just derived above, but modified to include the multiple passes required by the union of the results, and also the cost required to sort on QNAME. Accordingly, the complexity of this operation is limited to $O(n)$.

In summary, this analysis suggests that the potential best performance of the matching algorithm has linear complexity, $O(n)$. This compares favorably with the ERM described in Section 6, considering also that semantic matching is considered in the TSCM.

3. TSCM VS. FEDERATED DATABASE SYSTEMS: EXTENDING TRADITIONAL DATABASE INTEGRATION TECHNOLOGY

Federated Database Systems (FDBSs) are multi-database systems that are classified according to the degree to which the federation is distributed, heterogeneous and autonomous. They are classified as tightly-coupled if the administration of the federated schema is centralized and tightly controlled, and so local databases have reduced or no autonomy; or loosely-coupled if the database administration is distributed thus granting local databases greater autonomy. Databases in the federation may be homogenous where all databases share the same database schema, or may be heterogeneous requiring all databases to subscribe to a canonical data model. With respect to these definitions, the TSCM possesses a combination of both classifications. It requires centralized management of the global data model as represented by the Metadatabase, although there are efforts to support a distributed model (Hsu 1996). On the other hand, the publication and subscription query facility demonstrate the loosely-coupled qualities of the TSCM, which extends the degree of autonomy typically found in FDBSs. That is, export databases submit queries to the Blackboard when *active* participation in the federation is desired, which is contrary to the FDBS approach where component databases are beholden to an authority, centralized or otherwise, when it becomes a member of a federation. This autonomy difference is analyzed in greater detail in the next two sections.

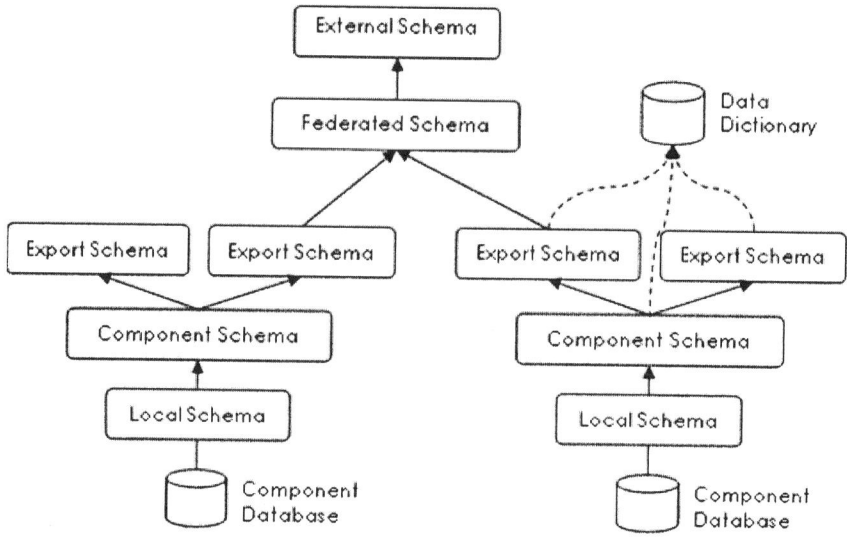

Figure 7-3. Five-schema Architecture of Federated Database Systems

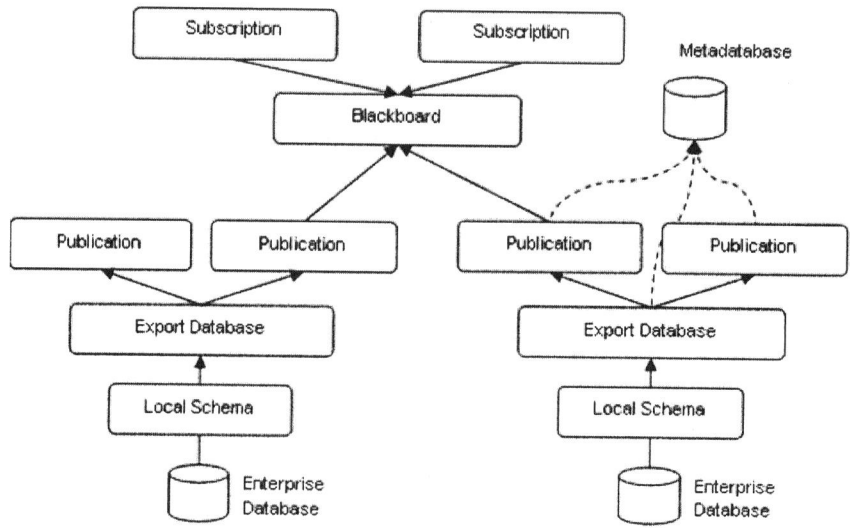

Figure 7-4. Four-schema Architecture of the TSCM

Figure 7-3 and Figure 7-4 illustrate the architecture of a FDBS and the TSCM respectively. The FDBS schema architecture is a five-schema architecture as opposed to the classical three-schema architecture, which does a better job of addressing database distribution, heterogeneity and autonomy. The TSCM shares a similar architecture; however the export schema is replaced with an export database and so we classify the TSCM architecture is classified as a four-schema architecture. The local schema belongs to the enterprise database and constitutes a single schema, while the export database data model is defined by the publication queries. Accordingly, the publication queries and the export database constitute one schema. The Blackboard meta-schema and the subscription queries constitute the remaining two schemas, which results in a four-schema architecture. The reduction in the number of schemas however does not correspond to a reduction in the degree of autonomy; rather the converse is true in this instance, since the export database in conjunction with the Blackboard provides an added dimension to the autonomy of the TSCM architecture.

This export database represents the fundamental difference between the traditional FDBS and the TSCM. It provides an opportunity to realize an increase in the autonomy of enterprise databases that participate in a TSCM, hereafter regarded as the federation, relative to traditional FDBSs. The combination of the export database and publication queries allows the enterprise database to participate in the federation, both *passively* and *actively*. *Passive* participation implies that the enterprise database is a member of the federation but does not actively participate in global query. Specifically, the enterprise data model, or a subset of this data model is registered with the Metadatabase, and no publication queries corresponding to the related export database reside at the Blackboard. On the other hand, *active* participation arises when queries have been submitted to the Blackboard, a corresponding export database has been defined, and the enterprise database is therefore actively engaged in the query matching process. The advantages of this approach are made evident when to discontinue participation in federation, a component database in a traditional FDBS would have to remove itself entirely from the federation to prevent access to its data sources, thus rendering the federated schema compromised.

Export databases, and the architecture of the TSCM in general also contribute to improving database distribution, by providing the opportunity to scale to significantly larger numbers of databases in the federation relative to traditional FDBSs. Scalability in the context of the TSCM pertains to the ability of the FDBS to add increasingly greater numbers of databases without loss of functionality and performance, but rather to take full advantage of the available database resources. However, as traditional

FDBSs grow larger, the management of the corresponding federated database management system (FDBMS) grows increasingly intractable. It therefore becomes increasingly difficult to manage the FDBMS, that is, to create/modify global database schemata or facilitate queries over multi-database systems, since a significant investment of time and human resources would be necessary to maintain the infrastructure. Indeed, traditional FDBSs were typically employed by enterprises, which were able to control and limit the scope of the federation. Conversely, the TSCM presents the opportunity for the federation to scale to significantly larger numbers of databases, since there is no rigid connection required between participating databases. The registration of the enterprise database schema into the Metadatabase still requires a manual effort, that is, conversion of the independent data models to global representation requires human input, which presents the single, although not crippling, bottleneck in this approach. With respect to other comparable schema integration approaches however, the Metadatabase in concert with the Blackboard facilitates an open and distributed administration regime, where enterprise databases independently control and manage access to their data resources.

4. TSCM VS. MULTI-AGENT SYSTEMS: THE TSCM AS A PLATFORM FOR IMPLEMENTING MULTI-AGENT SYSTEMS

Multi-Agent Systems (MASs) share a common mission with the TSCM, i.e. to address information sharing within distributed, heterogeneous and autonomous environments. However, these systems overlap with the TSCM primarily at the first stage, i.e., information matching. The RETSINA MAS (Sycara, Klusch et al. 1999; Sycara, Lu et al. 1999; Sycara, Paolucci et al. 2003) is one such solution to this research problem, which utilizes autonomous software agents as the drivers for information sharing. This process, known as matchmaking, uses a middle agent (matchmaker) to broker agent transactions between provider agents and requestor agents. Provider agents issue advertisements for services they provide, while requestor agents issue queries/requests to the middle agent for providers of services. The middle-agent stores all advertisements and provides these to the requestor agent upon request.

The challenge in the RETSINA MAS and MASs in general is to facilitate the interoperability of heterogeneous agents that possess various capabilities. The motivation of the RETSINA MAS has been to provide a neutral, domain independent infrastructure where heterogeneous agents can communicate and interoperate with each other. Towards this end, the

RETSINA infrastructure provides an Agent Communication Language (ACL) for describing advertisements and requests entitled the Language for Advertisements and Requests for Knowledge Sharing (LARKS). LARKS accounts for the capabilities of agents by including ontological references, keywords and descriptions in each specification. It is assumed that the ontologies supported by agents are rooted in a concept language ITL (Information Terminological Language), which leads to a further assumption that the semantics of the terminologies expressed in the ontologies are shared across MASs. The matching of requests to advertisements depends partially on the matching of these ontological expressions which is discussed next.

Table 7-3. Similarities between the TSCM and the RETSINA Multi-Agent System

TSCM	RETSINA MAS
Publication Query	Provider Agent
Subscription Query	Requestor Agent
Blackboard	Matchmaker Agent
exMQL	LARKS
Metadatabase	Combined Agent Ontology

The RETSINA MAS has adopted a number of methods to match request with advertisements, or the matching of specifications in general. In increasing order of complexity, the matching process offers (1) Context Matching, which restricts matching to specifications of the same domain, (2) Profile Comparison, which measures the degree of similarity between two specifications, (3) Similarity Matching, which compares the word distance between concepts expressed in the input/output declarations indicated in the specification, and (4) Signature matching, and (5) Constraint Matching, where both combined determine if the input/output declarations match. It will become evident the TSCM offers a simpler method to matchmaking, and in general a less complex approach to the problem of information sharing when compared to the RETSINA MAS. Table 7-3 illustrates the obvious similarities between the TSCM and RETSINA MAS.

The TSCM approach to matchmaking or query matching as described in Chapter 4 is considerably simpler than the corresponding matchmaking approach in the RETSINA MAS. The Blackboard serves as the broker between databases offering publication and subscription queries and performs a two-stage process to identify matches between these objects. As illustrated in Chapter 4, the first stage identifies matching queries that contain common data items and classifies the match according to the number of common items found in each match, i.e. exact match, superset/subset match, and intersect match. The second stage attempts to integrate/combine subset and intersect matches identified in the first stage such that they constitute a combination exact match, combination superset/subset match or combination intersect match. Since semantic differences have been resolved at design-time, when the schema of a new database has been added to the Metadatabase, then the TSCM relies on straightforward relational query processing to identify affected queries. The equivalence of queries therefore is determined by the heuristic algorithms described in Chapter 4. This first stage of query matching compares favorably with the approach to matchmaking in the RETSINA MAS. To the best of our knowledge the second stage of query matching has no counterpart in the RETSINA MAS, i.e. no discussion of agents working to together in the RETSINA MAS to satisfy a request from a requestor agent, although other MASs attempt to address this problem.

ExMQL also provides a concise representation method for publications and subscriptions as opposed to requests and advertisements in the RETSINA MAS.

AWAC-AirMissions	
Context	Combat, Mission*AWAC-AirMission
Types	Date = (mm: Int, dd: Int, yy: Int) DeployedMission = ListOf(mt: String, mid:String||Int, mStart: Date, mEnd: Date)
Input	start: Date, end: Date
Output	missions: DeployedMission;
InConstraints	start <= end.
OutConstraints	deployed(mID), mt = AWAC, launchedAfter(mid,mStart), launchedBefore(mID,mEnd).
ConcDescriptions	AWAC-AirMission = (and AirMission (atleast 1 has-airplane) (atmost 1 has-airplane) (all has-airplane aset(E-2)))
TextDescription	capable of providing information on deployed AWAC air combat missions launched in some given time interval

Figure 7-5. LARKS specification for Agent Advertisement (Sycara, Klusch et al. 1999)

Figure 7-5 and Table 7-4 illustrate an advertisement in LARKS and the corresponding publication in exMQL. The example illustrated in Table

7-4 assumes that the data items specified are attributes of the enterprise database schema, but as illustrated represent the global attributes as defined in the global data model. Recall that publication attributes are defined in terms of the global data model, as is the schema of the export database which corresponds to the publication query. Moreover, the export database data values are converted to their global equivalents via the equivalence functionality of the Metadatabase.

Table 7-4. Corresponding exMQL Publication for LARKS Advertisement illustrated in Fig. 7-5

```
PUT mID, mt, mStart, mEnd
FOR mStart = DATE
AND mEND = DATE
AND mStart <= mEND
AND mt = 'AWAC'
```

Therefore, while software agents are endowed with intelligence to make complex decisions, the implementation of these agents and the underlying multi-agent system is no simple task. The RETSINA MAS and other current results in the MAS field depend on heuristics to define the match methods and agent capabilities. These characteristics however differ across the various research efforts thus preventing interoperability and requiring custom solutions (Sycara, Klusch et al. 1999) to facilitate integration. In contrast query matching in the TSCM utilizes proven database technology with established standards; the methods of the TSCM are built using the PL/SQL facilities of a database management system, and so the limitations to the architecture are only constrained by the capabilities of the underlying software and hardware. As illustrated in Table 7-3, the similarities between the TSCM and the RETSINA MAS are extensive, which leads us to believe that the TSCM could be used as the platform on which the RETSINA MAS, and perhaps MASs in general could be built upon.

5. TSCM VS. SUPPLY-CHAIN INTEGRATION ARCHITECTURES: AN ARCHITECTURE FOR GLOBAL QUERY IN THE SUPPLY-CHAIN

EDI (Electronic Data Interchange) has long been the standard upon which supply-chain solutions have been built, but within the relatively recent past XML-based solutions have been used as substitutes to this long-standing approach. MESChain (Cingil and Dogac 2001) is a supply-chain integration architecture that employs emerging technologies and standards to facilitate electronic catalog interoperability, workflow process automation and other benefits. From this analysis of MESChain is discovered that supply-chain integration and automation warrants a database-oriented solution, but as yet no such solution has emerged to address this need, although MESChain does provide a compelling substitute. Consequently, the TSCM has been developed to fill this void, which is convincingly demonstrated in the examples in Chapter 6. The TSCM is a database-oriented solution that offers a number of advantages when compared to MESChain, ranging from a consistent integration platform where deviations from this approach are limited to messaging protocol alone, to the advanced integrity controls provided by database systems, which tightly integrate the data and operations made on them. In the analysis that follows we question specific contributions of MESChain, and compare these with the capabilities of the TSCM.

5.1 Interoperability of Distributed and Heterogeneous Suppliers in the Supply-Chain

Interoperability within MESChain is facilitated by the Common Business Library (CBL), which provides a canonical catalog description to which all merchants in the supply-chain subscribe. The transformation or mapping of the independent XML applications and documents in the supply-chain to the CBL ensures the semantic consistency of product catalogs. To participate therefore, each merchant in the supply-chain must adopt the information models which constitute the CBL, which in the end we believe is reminiscent of the rigid approach to schema integration in distributed database management systems. It is assumed however, that this process is embedded in wrapper programs that preserve the autonomy of the merchants, but this has not been explicitly stated.

In comparison, the interoperability of the TSCM is facilitated via the Metadatabase, which defines the global data model that is derived from the integration of databases schemas obtained from the participating enterprise databases. This global data model, its meta-structure (See the GIRD, Chapter 2) and the supporting database infrastructure is arguably a superior integration solution than that provided by the CBL. Firstly, the global data model is extensible, and will adapt to reflect new global data attributes as local database schemata are added to the Metadatabase, given the following additional advantage. Second, the management of the global data model is trivial, since the addition, deletion or modification of the schemas from the data model, correspond to traditional data manipulation languages: the insert, delete and update commands of a database management system, which incidentally does not require the database systems to be taken off-line. Finally, the meta-structure has proven to be enduring and robust for the applications in which is has been utilized (Hsu 1996) over the past decade.

5.2   Customized Views in the Supply-Chain

Customized product catalogs provide the ability to combine product descriptions from different merchants throughout the MESChain supply-chain. The benefits include a product catalog customized to a customers needs, and a catalog reflecting current product data. However, as indicated in (Cingil and Dogac 2001), this customization feature leads to a sub-optimal representation of the product catalog, since typically this introduces repetitive catalog information for each product description, which is necessary for the catalog to validate against the associated DTD.

In contrast, the TSCM subscription query facility provides essentially the same functionality as a MESChain customized catalog, but in a relatively concise format. The subscription query can include data from multiple export databases in the supply-chain, at any level in the supply-chain (See Chapter 6).

Figure 7-6 and Table 7-5 illustrate a customized catalog for a 300MHz desktop PC in MESChain and the corresponding subscription query in the TSCM, respectively. The query in Fig. 7-5 consists of three separate queries, and a function that includes two sub-queries, although only one query is executed if the other fails. However, the subscription query requires a single databases *select* query on the Blackboard in the first stage of query matching and an additional heuristic to classify the results, in order to identify matching publication queries, (See Chapter 4).

The query in Table 7-5 is valid given the following assertions: (1) the specified data attributes are globally defined, and are available in one or more publication queries, and (2) the literal value of the constraint is defined within the domain of the corresponding attribute. See Chapter 4 for additional information on the formulation of subscription and publication queries.

```
FUNCTION Get.Proddesc.General.Element (in $pdi, in $proddesc_url )
  { WHERE <product.description ident = "$pdi">
           <product.description.general> </> ELEMENT_AS $pdge
           </> IN $proddesc_url
     RETURN $pdge }
  { WHERE <product.description ident = "$pdi">
           <product.description.general.pointer ident = "$pdgi">
           <url.reference url.string = "$pdgidesc_url">
           </></></> IN $proddesc_url
     RETURN Get.Proddesc.General.Element($pdgi, $pdgidesc_url) }
END


WHERE <catalog>
       <catalog.entry.pointer ident = "$cei">
        <url.reference url.string = "$catentry_url">
       </></> ELEMENT_AS $cep_element
      </> IN "www.srdc.metu.edu.tr/sc/R1.catalog.xml",

       <catalog.entry ident = "$cei">
        <product.description.group>
         <product.description.pointer ident = "$pdi">
          <url.reference url.string = "$proddesc_url">
       </></></></> IN "$catentry_url",

       <product.description.general>
        <keyword.set><keyword>Desktop</></>
         <feature.set> <feature.group>
          <feature.name>Clock Speed</>
          <feature.name.value><mhz>$mhz_value</></>
       </></></> IN Get.Proddesc.General.Element($pdi, $proddesc_url),

       EXPR "($mhz_value >= 300)"

 CONSTRUCT $cep_element INTO "result1.xml"
```

Figure 7-6. An XML Query in MESChain (Cingil and Dogac 2001)

Table 7-5. An exMQL Subscription Query that Corresponds to the XML Query in Fig. 7-6

```
GET desktop clock_speed mhz_value
FOR mhz_value >= 300
```

5.3   Traversal of the Supply-Chain

Visibility in the supply-chain is generally limited to the customer's immediate supplier(s) or purchaser(s). As illustrated in Chapter 6 however, a supplier may be connected to one supplier, or more. MESChain provides the opportunity to "drill down" these supply-chains, to view the catalog of a supplier, and the supplier's supplier(s) and so on. This is facilitated through a specification of links in the product catalog: "up-links" that are linked to purchasers, and "down-links," which are linked to suppliers. This functionality allows a customer the ability to navigate the MESChain using a product property as a pivot point (such as a product brand), which allows the customer to identify the suppliers, retailers, and manufacturers and so on that also feature the product.

A similar, but more robust feature is available in the TSCM. The global data model describes the global knowledge of all connected databases. Moreover, the Blackboard describes the particular global knowledge that is offered for consumption in the supply-chain. The exMGQS (See Chapter 5) provides the opportunity to navigate the Blackboard and to interact with the offered subscription and publication queries. The *vertical traversal* of the Blackboard allows the user to navigate to a particular export database, and interact with the publication queries that define this resource. The *horizontal traversal* on the other hand allows the user to choose a specific data item within a publication query, and pivot about this object to identify the related queries and correspondingly, the export databases that contain this global data item. Accordingly, this avails a user of the opportunity to see how the particular data item is utilized, and to what other data items/objects to which it is connected. This facility to enable this functionality is derived from the initial modeling effort when an enterprise database schema is integrated in the global data model. The declaration of the attributes in the enterprise schema that correspond to the global attributes automatically establishes the connections with the other enterprise databases in the supply-chain. The availability of subscription and publications at the Blackboard, which contain these global data items, therefore establishes the links between suppliers and consumers and so affirms the robustness of this approach, in contrast to MESChain where these links will have to be declared manually for each connected resource.

6. TSCM VS. ERM: A GLOBAL QUERY APPROACH TO AGENT TASK MATCHING

The TSCM shares the same goals and basic concepts with the Enterprises Resources Market model; however, the ERM is more a general conceptual design than a complete technology that is ready for testing or even for implementation. In a sense, the TSCM reduces the basic concept of ERM to practice with a particular method of information matching – i.e., developing an artificial market to facilitate the collaboration of databases, with the possibility of considering pricing and other measures of value to determine an optimal allocation of resources. As indicated in this research, the TSCM is concerned more specifically with the on-demand information exchange that enterprise collaboration requires, and seeks more directly to expand the realm of the previous global query of databases.

Technically speaking, a significant point between these two models - and the one we focus on in this analysis - is the Blackboard design. Whereas the design with the ERM facilitates the matching of agent tasks, the design with the TSCM optimizes the matching of queries. The two designs could be considered as two competing approaches; or, more preferably as the view we adopted, the query-based design in TSCM is interpreted as a particular method for constructing the task agents in the ERM. With the latter view, the Blackboard of the TSCM is the Match Engine of the ERM that facilitates agent transactions, and is coupled with a database (the query database) to store tasks (the queries). The difference is that agents in the general literature (and hence in the ERM design) are assumed to be realized with software threads, which search the repository of agents (often a flat file) for matching tasks. An agent determines a match by using an internal evaluation function to determine the goodness of fit. A simple example of an internal evaluation function could be price and time; the requestor agent pays a certain price X to a provider agent within a given time period. Consequently, if a match is found the corresponding sleeping threads are alerted, which when bound together with the matching thread, form a run-time agent. If a match is not found, then the software thread (Agent) is put to sleep, and the corresponding task is placed in the database. In a laboratory testing of a particular software agent design for the ERM model (see Hsu, et.al. 2006), the architecture of the Agent-Base can support upwards of 100,000 agents on a single machine, and upwards of millions of agents across a distributed network of databases.

When compare the prevalent agent design in the literature against the database approach of the TSCM, the significant difference is the richness of the matching logic, which happens to have advantages on either platform. The Blackboard in the TSCM by virtue of the integration with the

Metadatabase offers the semantic matching of queries. The Blackboard in the ERM does not possess this capability. Moreover, the Blackboard in the TSCM simply performs the matching of queries which may consist of the evaluation of meta-attributes that describe market variables, but otherwise does not implement a market. The market approach is a novel one, allowing market dynamics to determine the value of goods and services. The ERM provides this functionality through the internal evaluation functions that are native to each agent. Therefore, this matching is flexible and adaptive, but nonetheless suffers the problem that is endemic in current technologies in which semantic matching is questionable.

The TSCM also offers an extensible architecture, by virtue of the complete implementation in a RDBMS. This lends itself to the notion of database independence that the database provides for applications. Similarly, by providing a generic matching protocol, the Blackboard and new market-based technologies can build on these resources, ignoring the underlying implementation, and focusing on the functional aspects of these applications.

Chapter 8

WHERE DO WE STAND?

1.   A REVIEW OF THE RESULTS

The existing solutions for information exchange in the supply-chain are limited. They allow for document and message exchange and so only scratch the surface when considering collaboration in the TSCM, given the volume of information in enterprise databases that are available for sharing. Likewise, traditional global database query has the potential to revolutionize information exchange in the supply-chain, but to do so it must shed the restrictive requirements it places on member databases, and embrace the open architectures of the virtual enterprise. The TSCM evolves information exchange in the enterprise; it extends the traditional global query paradigm and allows for the conditional participation of databases in the information exchange. Moreover, it empowers databases to consider exactly what information is shared from their data resources, in contrast to traditional approaches where the participation by default determines and controls what is shared. The global query process has also been extended in the TSCM, which introduces a bi-directional global query process, whereas the traditional approach is unidirectional. Traditional global query only considers the user side; queries are executed against a fixed set of databases, and so it does not consider the needs of the database. Indeed, the database should retain the capability to determine who to associate with, and what information to share, in addition to publishing their data resources so that information seekers are brought to the attention of the information that is available.

To realize the benefits of the TSCM, a new global query architecture consisting of the Blackboard, Export Database Shell, described in Chapter 5, and the Metadatabase (See Chapter 2) has been developed. The Blackboard provides for the large-scale concurrent processing and matching of queries, which is realized in a general-purpose relational database management system. The Blackboard determines matches between information requests and offers, which are provided by data subscribers and data publishers respectively. Following a query matching session (See Chapter 6), the execution of the query is assigned to the export database associated with the winning data publisher for processing. The Export Database Shell integrates enterprise databases into the TSCM via the creation of the export database, and so does not compromise the heterogeneity and autonomy of these databases. The publication of an information offer initiates the creation of a corresponding export database views in the export database, which reflects the data retrieved from the enterprise database. The interface to the enterprise database is realized through the enterprise database monitor that is unique for each export database shell and is dependent on the particular hardware and software utilized at the site. The enterprise database monitor periodically updates the export database to keep the data current, on a schedule determined by the policies of the enterprise domain. The Metadatabase is the fundamental element in the design of the TSCM that acknowledges the distributed knowledge, i.e. the operating and decision rules in the distributed systems. It integrates the schemata of the distributed systems into a single global data model to facilitate global query that is system transparent, and performance-wise indifferent to the autonomy, heterogeneity of the distributed databases (See Chapter 2).

The contributions of this research are the query matching algorithms, the design of the architecture for the Blackboard and Export Database, the Extended Global Query Language (exMQL), and the Extended Metadatabase Global Query System (exMGQS). Three algorithms pertaining to the Blackboard were developed in this research (See Chapter 4). The first algorithm, Matching identifies matching queries in the Blackboard given a supplied query. For example, given an information request the Matching algorithm iterates through the query database of the Blackboard and compares the data items of each information offer that it finds with the data items in the information request. If it identifies an information offer that contains data items common to the information request then it classifies the match according to the number of data items that are found. An offer that contains the same items as the request, which includes quantity and semantics, is denoted as an exact match. If the request is a subset of the offer, then it is denoted a subset match. If the request is a superset of the offer then it is denoted a superset match, and finally if they contain common items but do not meet the aforementioned criteria then the match is denoted an intersect match.

A second round of processing takes place if no exact or subset matches are found. In this case, the Combination Matching algorithm is executed taking as inputs the queries classified as superset and intersect matches. The Combination Matching algorithm generates the set of combinations these queries and determines if the combination provides a solution for the information request. In this regard, the algorithm determines combination exact, combination superset, combination subset and combination intersect matches. The combination exact and combination subset are the only categories of relevance. In this case, these two categories are denoted item feasible, if they contain the necessary items to match the information request. It is necessary however to determine if the combination is join feasible, i.e. if the queries constituting the combination query are logically connected. If the disparate queries contain common items then a query join operation can be performed, and so the combination query is considered join feasible.

In the event the queries are not logically connected then the Metadatabase is consulted to determine if a solution can found. In this regard, a modified Shortest Path Algorithm (See Appendix A) searches the Metadatabase for data items that will logically connect the queries. If a solution is found, it will return a set of data items required to connect the combination query. Since the data items are not apart of the original combination query, then it is necessary to modify the affected queries, and so the system alerts the affected data publishers and/or data subscribers. Given a join feasible solution, the third algorithm is executed.

The Constraint Matching algorithm (See Chapter 4) determines the constraint feasibility of queries by determining if the constraints in the queries are compatible. Since it is not possible to evaluate actual data values, the algorithm instead uses truth tables to asses the truth value of the constraints. The export databases that correspond to the queries that are item, join and constraint feasible are then allocated the supplied query, and the supplied query is then delivered to the appropriate export databases for processing. In the event that multiple query matches are found, such as in the case of multiple publication queries for a single subscription query, then the Blackboard applies the decision criteria provided in the queries, or automatically applies these criteria if they are not included in the queries. Finally, given an acceptable solution, the query is executed on the affected export databases.

2. COMPARATIVE PROPERTIES

We analyze further the properties of the TSCM. The model is unique in the two-stage concept, the information matching method, and the creation of the Export Database as a direct participant (in contrast to an export schema of a participant). Together, they have the promise to turn the traditional one-to-many rigid command relationship between users and databases into one that is many-to-many and ad hoc. The new relationship is unprecedented in the Global Database Query literature. Moreover, the TSCM improves the properties of the Metadatabase model, and other similar results in the literature (see Chapter 1), concerning autonomy, heterogeneity, and openness and scalability of integration, by virtue of developing the new first stage.

The TSCM expands local autonomy by affording participants the ability to connect and disconnect from the global query infrastructure at will. In traditional global query systems, including the Metadatabase, a distributed database is always available for global database query. The databases cannot control when and how their data resources are utilized, unless the local data model is removed entirely from the global query infrastructure. The TSCM separates the registration structure from the global query architecture, as represented by the Metadatabase and Blackboard respectively. A local database participates in global query only when the data to be shared is made public, by submitting queries to the Blackboard. Otherwise, the local database remains a part of the global community, but does not participate in its information exchange.

Heterogeneity is another limit with the traditional global query methods that the TSCM improves. Previous results tend to accommodate local heterogeneity by relying on some kind of a global administrator, whose limits, therefore, represent the limits on the heterogeneity. The Metadatabase model, for example, affords participating databases the ability to maintain a heterogeneous local schema by availing the Metadatabase to transform all global queries into an equivalent local query format via ROPE shells, which encapsulate the local databases. The TSCM expands heterogeneity in two ways. First, it provides an enterprise database monitor to the export database, to present the local data values and attributes in their equivalent global representation for all participants to see and use. This ability eases the burden of data conversion at the global site and thereby makes it easier to accommodate heterogeneous local systems. Second, the exMQL includes rules for the participants to declare constraints at the query level; which adds a degree of the heterogeneity accommodated.

Openness and scalability of integration was not a significant concern to traditional databases since the number of databases in an integration environment tended to be small. However, this is no longer the case with new practices such as supply chain integration. The Metadatabase allows a comparatively favorable degree of openness and scalability in the field, in that the addition, deletion, and modification of local data models are realized as ordinary database operations to the Metadatabase. So, member databases can be added, deleted and modified with relative ease. The TSCM expands the scalability since the Export Database shells facilitate the addition of diverse database systems and alternative data sources. It also maintains the openness of the Metadatabase model since it requires only the standard technology or even the open sources. The primary implementation effort is the development of wrappers to retrieve data from the enterprise databases, and the transformation of the resident data from the native format to the global format.

3.   OPPORTUNITIES FOR CONTINUING WORK

The TSCM results, including the design, the algorithms, and the prototype, are complete as a research solution and are ready for testing in practical settings. However, from the research perspective, continuing work is envisioned. Although the critical components of the TSCM have been established, there are number of areas that have not been completely implemented in the laboratory prototype. Moreover, there are a number of issues that need to be resolved before the TSCM is fully realized. Before looking at these issues, two alternative methods to implement the query matching algorithms are explored, in an effort to improve the overall performance of the Blackboard Match Engine.

First, as currently implemented the combination algorithm performs an exhaustive search of the Blackboard to evaluate combination queries. If the number of queries that match the supplied query is large then this can create a bottleneck in the query matching process. It has been determined that two approaches can be taken to alleviate this concern, (1) a divide and conquer strategy, and (2) a greedy strategy.

In the divide and conquer strategy, the combination query that considers all superset and intersect queries is evaluated, to determine if the combination query is item feasible. If it is, then the combination query is recursively split until one with the least number of queries is found, while still being item feasible. It then would be tested for join feasibility. If the join feasibility test fails then the algorithm backtracks and evaluates the previously discarded, item feasible, combination queries.

In the greedy strategy, the combination query that contains the greater number of data items that are common to the supplied query is considered, and the remaining queries and iteratively append to it, in an attempt to improve the item feasibility of the combination query. Once an item feasible solution is found, then the join feasibility is assessed

Furthermore, finding a better way to integrate the results from multiple export databases, rather than having this centralized at the Blackboard, will go far to improving the performance of the TSCM. Alternative methods to the approach implemented in this research include performing the integration of multiple query results at the export database shell, as opposed to the Blackboard. This would require that the Blackboard provide the relevant integration script to the affected export database, but this can be performed at the same time the queries are allocated to the export database.

With regards to completing the TSCM, the Blackboard and its attendant methods, the exMGQS and exMQL have been successfully implemented. Furthermore, the export database shell has been designed however, this has not been implemented. Moreover, the message protocol required to deliver exMQL queries to the export databases and back to the Blackboard, although alluded to in the research this has not been implemented. However, the requirements in this regard are easily met with current technologies, including for example SOAP (Simple Object Access Protocol) (W3C 2005) and XML-RPC (Remote Procedure Call) (Userland Software 2005), among others.

Additional work must also be performed to implement the functionality of publication queries creating views in an export database. The export database can be implemented on standard relational database technologies, and so the ability to create views is a trivial matter. However, translating the exMQL publication query into this SQL representation is another matter. First, the database views must be named such that these correspond to the query identifier, which should be unique both at the export database and at the Blackboard. It is this identifier that the Blackboard refers to when the query is to be allocated, and so must be unique to prevent conflicts at the export database. Furthermore, the methods by which these views are created must be investigated. What are the arrangements of the database tables? Are database tables' better alternatives to view creation, and must multiple tables be created to support each view, and accordingly each publication query, or is there a better solution?

The enterprise database monitor – the mechanism required to connect the enterprise database to the TSCM, has also been discussed. The enterprise database monitor facilitates populating the export database according to the attributes of the publication query, as well as the periodic updates of the export database given changes in the enterprise databases. It also transforms the enterprise data values and attributes into their global equivalents prior to being entered into the export database. This has not implemented or a design provided for this component, but this can be realized as a software wrapper that is custom designed for each enterprise database. Examples of this approach are seen in other database integration technologies such as Garlic (Carey, Haas et al. 1995).

This implementation of the TSCM considers user interactions with the database and vice versa, although the implications are database-to-database interaction. While there are solutions that approximate this functionality, for example, database replication, none addresses the need where a database autonomously interacts with another database. The ability of databases to autonomously publish their information contents with other databases facilitates the real-time management of data. Data in the collaboration is kept current without human intervention. This however leads to a concern which was not addressed in this research but does require exploration to ensure the completeness of exMQL. Specifically, this refers to the data management capabilities of exMQL. While this research has provided the methods to manipulate the data residing in the Blackboard, it has not explored the issue of managing content on an enterprise database. That is, can the export database be used as the conduit to maintain the information in enterprise databases? Is it possible, for an information request to be reinterpreted as an information update/delete/insert, such that upon submission to the Blackboard, the affected export database shells are notified and update/delete/insert their export databases and accordingly the enterprise databases. Being able to implement this functionality presents a tremendous opportunity to manage distributed information, which although previously addressed in the related literature (Babin 1993), is still bound to the traditional global query technology thus limiting its scope. By returning to one of the initial examples in the Introduction the benefits of such a framework can be realized. In homeland security; the sharing of information would no longer be a significant undertaking, since this dynamic database-to-database exchange would keep collaborating database up to date, semantically consistent and synchronized.

Appendix

1. THE OPERATIONAL ELEMENTS OF THE TWO-STAGE COLLABORATION MODEL

1.1 Extended Metadatabase Query Language (XML)

The XML syntax and diagrams illustrated in Figs. A-1 to A-16 uses the alternative BNF format described in (Babin 2004). This specification describes the operational query language of the TSCM. All queries in the current implementation are encoded in this message format.

- ```
  <exMQL> ::= '<exmql>' [<QUERY> | <DELETE_QUERY> |
  <DELETE_RULE>      |      <DELETE_CONDITION>      |
  <UPDATE_QUERY> ] '</exmql>' ;
  ```

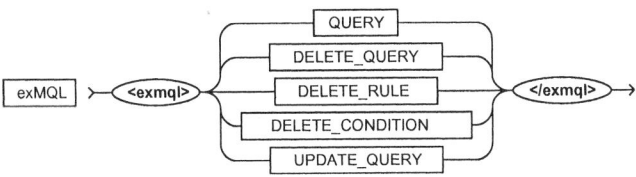

Figure A-1. exMQL QUERY Clause

- ```
  <QUERY> ::= '<query' <COMMAND> '>' <ITEMS> -[
  '<condlist>' +[<CONDITIONS>]+ '</condlist>' ]- -[
  '<actionlist>' +[ <ACTIONS>]+ '</actionlist>' ]-
  '</query>';
  ```

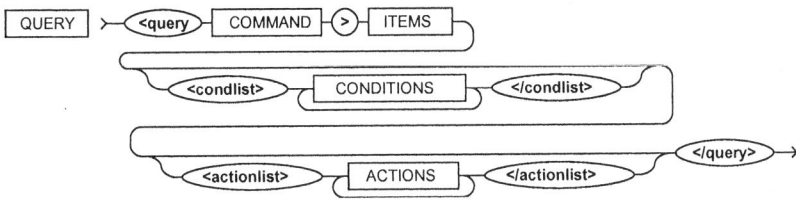

Figure A-2. exMQL QUERY Clause

152

- `<ITEMS> ::= '<items>' +[ '<item>' item '</item>' ]+ '</items>' ;`

Figure A-3. exMQL ITEMS Clause

- `<COMMAND> ::= 'command' '=' '"' [ 'get' | 'put' ] '"' ;`

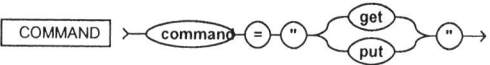

Figure A-4. exMQL QUERY COMMAND options

- `<CONDITIONS> ::= '<conds>' /[ <CONDITION> || <CONJOIN> ]/ '</conds>';`

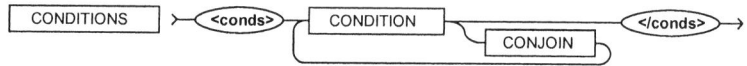

Figure A-5. exMQL CONDITIONS Clause

- `<CONJOIN> ::= '<conjoin op=' '"' [ 'and' | 'or' ] '"' '/>' ;`

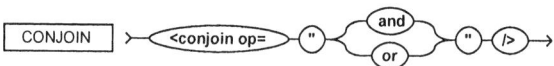

Figure A-6. exMQL CONJOIN options

- `<CONDITION> ::= '<cond ' [ <SELECT> | <JOIN> | <NEGOTIATE> ] '/>';`

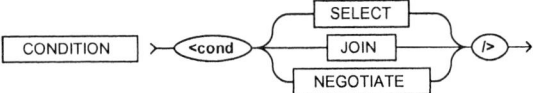

Figure A-7. exMQL CONDITION options

- `<SELECT> ::= 'loper' '=' '"' item '"' <BOUND> 'roper' '=' '"' value '"' ;`

Figure A-8. exMQL SELECTION Clause

- `<JOIN> ::= 'loper' '=' '"' item '"' <BOUND> 'roper' '=' '"' item '"' ;`

Figure A-9. exMQL JOIN Clause

- `<NEGOTIATE> ::= 'loper' '=' '"' parameter '"' <BOUND> 'roper' '=' '"' value '"' ;`

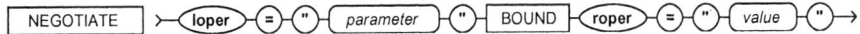

Figure A-10. exMQL NEGOTIATE Clause

- `<BOUND> ::= 'op' '=' '"' [ 'neq' | 'eq' | 'lt' | 'gt' | 'leq' | 'geq' ] '"' ;`

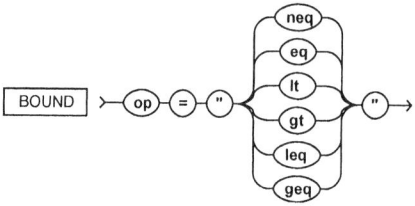

Figure A-11. exMQL BOUND options

- `<ACTIONS> ::= '<actions>' +[ '<action>' action '</action>' ]+ '</actions>' ;`

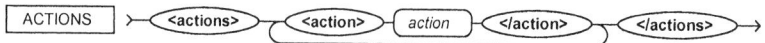

Figure A-12. exMQL ACTIONS Clause

- `<DELETE_QUERY> ::= '<delete' 'id' '=' '"' query_name '"' -[ 'isCascade' '=' '"' [ 'true' | 'false' ] '"' ]- '/>' ;`

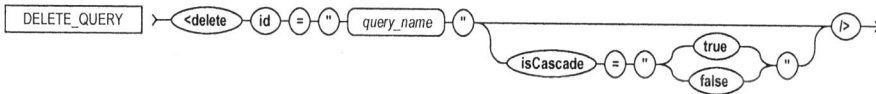

Figure A-13. exMQL DELETE QUERY Clause

- `<DELETE_RULE> ::= '<delete' 'id' '=' '"' query_name '"' '>' '<rules>' +[ '<rule' 'id' '=' '"' rule_name '"' '/>' ]+ '</rules>' '</delete>' ;`

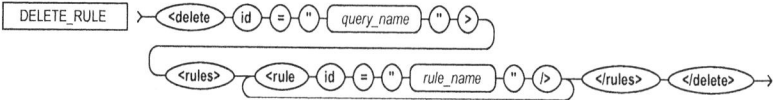

Figure A-14. exMQL DELETE RULE Clause

- `<DELETE_CONDITION>` `::=` `'<delete'` `'id'` `'='` `'"'`
  `query_name` `'"'` `'>'` `'<conds>'` `+[` `'<cond'` `'id'` `'='`
  `'"'` `condition_name` `'"'` `'/>'` `]+` `'</conds>'`
  `'</delete>'` `;`

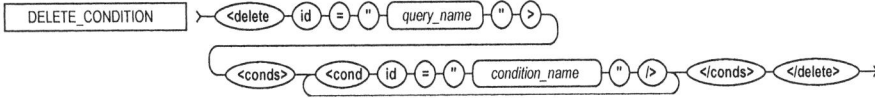

Figure A-15. exMQL DELETE CONDITION Clause

- `<UPDATE>` `::=` `'<update'` `'id'` `'='` `'"'` `query_name`
  `'"'` `'>'` `<ITEMS>` `:` `-[` `'<condlist>'`
  `+[<CONDITIONS>]+` `'</condlist>'` `]-` `-[`
  `'<actionlist>'` `+[` `<ACTIONS>]+` `'</actionlist>` `]-`
  `'</update>';`

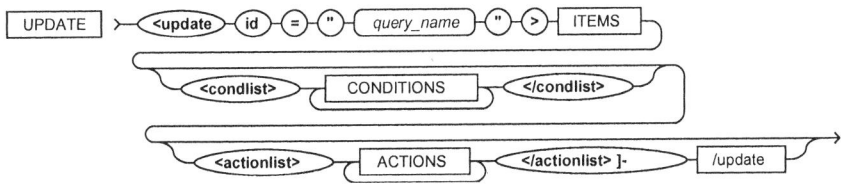

Figure A-16. exMQL UPDATE QUERY Clause

1.2   Modified Shortest Path Algorithm

The Shortest Path Algorithm below is derived from (Cheung 1991) and is included here to illustrate the slight modification, which is emboldened, required for the use in the TSCM. For the complete details of the operation of the TSCM, please see (Cheung 1991).

Table A-1. **Algorithm 1**: Shortest Path Algorithm (S)

Let *currentCost*: the current cost of the solution
Let *createMessage(A)*: Create a message for each node in A, where a message contains a unique identity, the cost and an indicator from which node the message is sent.
Let *currentCycle*: the set of messages that are currently being sent in the algorithm
Let *nextCycle*: the set of messages to be sent in the next round
Let *visitedNotes(S)*: the set of nodes that have previously received messages.
Let *numberCycle(S)*: the current cycle in the algorithm.
Let N^o: the set of nodes to be connected, where each node is a structure that has a key, the name of the node, the number of messages received and the set of messages it carries.
Let *root*: the current best solution of the algorithm
Let *newBestSolution()*: determines the solution is better than the previous solution
Let m_i: the ith message
Let n_j: the jth node

Function *determineShortestPath(N^o)*
currentCost $\leftarrow \infty$
root $\leftarrow \varnothing$
createMessage(N^o);
currentCycle(N^o);
nextCycle $\leftarrow \varnothing$
visitedNodes(N^o);
numberCycle $\leftarrow 1$

For (*currentCost < numberNodes – 1*)

    For each m_i in *currentCycle*
      listOfNodes = getRelatedEntrel($m_i \rightarrow$from)
  For each *node n_j* in *listofNodes*
If $n_j \notin$ *visitedNodes*
  $m_i \rightarrow from = m_i \rightarrow from + 1$;
  $m_i \rightarrow from = n_j \rightarrow key$;
  add m_i to *nextCycle*;
End-If
      If $m_i \notin n_j$
        add *message m_i* to n_j
        If *newBestSolution()*
          root = n_j
          currentCost = calculatedCost();
        End-If
      End-If
    End-For
  End-For
currentCycle = nextCycle
nextCycle $\leftarrow \varnothing$
nbCycle = nbCycle + 1;
End-For

End-Function

2. THE STRUCTURAL ELEMENTS OF THE METADATABASE AND THE BLACKBOARD

2.1 The DDL for the Blackboard

```
********************************************************************
**                                                              **
**                  FILE:  BLACKBOARD.DDL                       **
**      DDL STATEMENTS FOR CREATING THE BLACKBOARD DB MODEL     **
**                     IN POSTGRESQL                            **
**                                                              **
********************************************************************

-- ** Represents the users in an enterprise **
CREATE TABLE "USER"
        (USERID        CHARACTER VARYING(10) NOT NULL,
        LASTNAME       CHARACTER VARYING(20),
        FIRSTNAME      CHARACTER VARYING(20),
        POSITION       CHARACTER VARYING(40),
        PHONE          CHARACTER VARYING(14),
        OFFICE         CHARACTER VARYING(10),
        ADDRESS        CHARACTER VARYING(45),
        ADDEDBY        CHARACTER VARYING(10),
        DATEADDED      CHARACTER VARYING(10),
        MODIFBY        CHARACTER VARYING(10),
        LASTMOD        CHARACTER VARYING(10),
        NUMMODS        INTEGER,
        EMAIL          CHARACTER VARYING(60),
        SKILL          INTEGER);


-- ** Represents the systems of an enterprise **
CREATE TABLE SYSTEM (
        SYSNAME        CHARACTER VARYING(100) NOT NULL,
        DESCRIPT       CHARACTER VARYING(45),
        APPLCODE       CHARACTER VARYING(3),
        USERID         CHARACTER VARYING(10),
        ADDEDBY        CHARACTER VARYING(10),
        DATEADDED      CHARACTER VARYING(10),
        MODIFBY        CHARACTER VARYING(10),
        LASTMOD        CHARACTER VARYING(10),
        NUMMODS        INTEGER,
    IPADDRESS     CHARACTER VARYING(10),
    TIMESTAMP     TIMESTAMP);
```

```
-- ** Represents the views or subjects in a system **
CREATE TABLE QUERY (
        QNAME           CHARACTER VARYING(100) NOT NULL,
        DESCRIPT        CHARACTER VARYING(45),
        XCOORD          INTEGER,
        YCOORD          INTEGER,
        SYSNAME         CHARACTER VARYING(20),
        FILEID          CHARACTER VARYING(10),
        ADDEDBY         CHARACTER VARYING(10),
        DATEADDED       CHARACTER VARYING(10),
        MODIFBY         CHARACTER VARYING(10),
        LASTMOD         CHARACTER VARYING(10),
        NUMMODS         INTEGER,
   QTYPE        CHARACTER VARYING(10),
   TIMESTAMP      TIMESTAMP);

-- ** Represents the operational entity*relationships in an
enterprise **
CREATE TABLE VIEW (
        VNAME           CHARACTER VARYING(100) NOT NULL,
        DESCRIPT        CHARACTER VARYING(45),
        AKEY            CHARACTER VARYING(100),
        ADDEDBY         CHARACTER VARYING(10),
        DATEADDED       CHARACTER VARYING(10),
        MODIFBY         CHARACTER VARYING(10),
        LASTMOD         CHARACTER VARYING(10),
        NUMMODS         INTEGER);

-- ** Represents the structural integrity in a system **
CREATE TABLE INTEGRITY (
        INTNAME         CHARACTER VARYING(40) NOT NULL,
        INTTYPE         CHARACTER VARYING(2),
        DESCRIPT        CHARACTER VARYING(45),
        MASTER          CHARACTER VARYING(40),
        SLAVE           CHARACTER VARYING(40),
        ADDEDBY         CHARACTER VARYING(10),
        DATEADDED       CHARACTER VARYING(10),
        MODIFBY         CHARACTER VARYING(10),
        LASTMOD         CHARACTER VARYING(10),
        NUMMODS         INTEGER);

-- ** Represents the data items in an enterprise **
CREATE TABLE ITEM (
        ITEMCODE        CHARACTER VARYING(100) NOT NULL,
        ITEMNAME        CHARACTER VARYING(40),
        ITEMTYPE        INTEGER,
        DESCRIPT        CHARACTER VARYING(45),
        IFORMAT         CHARACTER VARYING(20),
```

```
        ILENGTH         INTEGER,
        PRECISION       INTEGER,
        DOMAIN          CHARACTER VARYING(20),
        UNIT            CHARACTER VARYING(20),
        DEFVALUE        CHARACTER VARYING(20),
        SYSNAME         CHARACTER VARYING(20),
        ADDEDBY         CHARACTER VARYING(10),
        DATEADDED       CHARACTER VARYING(10),
        MODIFBY         CHARACTER VARYING(10),
        LASTMOD         CHARACTER VARYING(10),
        NUMMODS         INTEGER);

-- ** Represents the contextual knowledge within or across the
systems **
CREATE TABLE CONTEXT (
        CNAME           CHARACTER VARYING(20) NOT NULL,
        DESCRIPT        CHARACTER VARYING(45),
        XCOORD          INTEGER,
        YCOORD          INTEGER,
        SYSNAME         CHARACTER VARYING(20),
        ADDEDBY         CHARACTER VARYING(10),
        DATEADDED       CHARACTER VARYING(10),
        MODIFBY         CHARACTER VARYING(10),
        LASTMOD         CHARACTER VARYING(10),
        NUMMODS         INTEGER);

-- ** Represents the production rules used in a subject or
context **
CREATE TABLE RULE (
        RNAME           CHARACTER VARYING(20) NOT NULL,
        RTYPE           CHARACTER VARYING(20),
        DESCRIPT        CHARACTER VARYING(45),
        CONDID          CHARACTER VARYING(10),
        NUMBCONDS       INTEGER,
        ADDEDBY         CHARACTER VARYING(10),
        DATEADDED       CHARACTER VARYING(10),
        MODIFBY         CHARACTER VARYING(10),
        LASTMOD         CHARACTER VARYING(10),
        NUMMODS         INTEGER);

-- ** Represents the action part of a rule **
CREATE TABLE ACTION
        (ACTID          CHARACTER VARYING(10) NOT NULL,
        ACTTYPE         INTEGER,
        FACTID          CHARACTER VARYING(10),
        DECLVALUE       CHARACTER VARYING(1));

-- ** Table containing the facts used by the rule processor **
CREATE TABLE FACT
```

```
        (FACTID         CHARACTER VARYING(10) NOT NULL,
        FACTNAME        CHARACTER VARYING(80),
        DESCRIPT        CHARACTER VARYING(45),
        FACTTYPE        INTEGER,
        FACTVALUE       CHARACTER VARYING(20),
        VALUETYPE       CHARACTER VARYING(20),
        VALUEOF         CHARACTER VARYING(10),
        BINDTYPE        INTEGER);

-- ** Represents the condition part of a rule **
CREATE TABLE CONDITION (
        CONDID          CHARACTER VARYING(10) NOT NULL,
        LEFTFACT        CHARACTER VARYING(10),
        OPERATOR        CHARACTER VARYING(10),
        RIGHTFACT       CHARACTER VARYING(10));

-- ** Represents the hardware resources (systems) used in an
enterprise **
CREATE TABLE HARDWARE_RESOURCE (
        SERIALNO        CHARACTER VARYING(100) NOT NULL,
        HNAME           CHARACTER VARYING(20),
        HTYPE           CHARACTER VARYING(20),
        DESCRIPT        CHARACTER VARYING(45),
        LOCATION        CHARACTER VARYING(20),
        NODENAME        CHARACTER VARYING(20),
        NODEADDR        CHARACTER VARYING(20),
        MANUFACTURER    CHARACTER VARYING(40),
        PURCHBY         CHARACTER VARYING(40),
        DATEPURCH       CHARACTER VARYING(10),
        USERID          CHARACTER VARYING(10),
        ADDEDBY         CHARACTER VARYING(10),
        DATEADDED       CHARACTER VARYING(10),
        MODIFBY         CHARACTER VARYING(10),
        LASTMOD         CHARACTER VARYING(10),
        NUMMODS         INTEGER);

-- ** The software resources (files, programs, and documents)
used by the systems **
CREATE TABLE SOFTWARE_RESOURCE (
        RESID           CHARACTER VARYING(100) NOT NULL,
        RESNAME         CHARACTER VARYING(40),
        EXTENSION       CHARACTER VARYING(3),
        RESTYPE         CHARACTER VARYING(20),
        DESCRIPT        CHARACTER VARYING(45),
        SIZEVALUE       INTEGER,
        SIZEUNIT        CHARACTER VARYING(20),
        CODING          CHARACTER VARYING(20),
        DEVELOPBY       CHARACTER VARYING(45),
        ADDEDBY         CHARACTER VARYING(10),
```

```
        DATEADDED       CHARACTER VARYING(10),
        MODIFBY         CHARACTER VARYING(10),
        LASTMOD         CHARACTER VARYING(10),
        NUMMODS         INTEGER);

-- ** A PR between SYSTEM and USER entities **
CREATE TABLE SYSTEMUSER
        (SYSNAME        CHARACTER VARYING(20) NOT NULL,
        USERID          CHARACTER VARYING(10) NOT NULL,
        UPASSWORD       CHARACTER VARYING(10),
        SKILL           INTEGER,
        ACCESSCODE      CHARACTER VARYING(2),
        ADDEDBY         CHARACTER VARYING(10),
        DATEADDED       CHARACTER VARYING(10),
        MODIFBY         CHARACTER VARYING(10),
        LASTMOD         CHARACTER VARYING(10),
        NUMMODS         INTEGER);

-- ** A PR between SYSTEM and SOFTWARE entities **
CREATE TABLE USES
        (SYSNAME        CHARACTER VARYING(100) NOT NULL,
        RESID           CHARACTER VARYING(100) NOT NULL,
        DATAORG         CHARACTER VARYING(20));

-- ** A PR between VIEW and SYSTEM entities **
CREATE TABLE NAMEDAS
        (VNAME          CHARACTER VARYING(100) NOT NULL,
        SYSNAME         CHARACTER VARYING(100) NOT NULL,
        LOCALNAME       CHARACTER VARYING(40));

-- ** A recursive PR on SOFTWARE entity **
CREATE TABLE MODULEOF
        (SUBRESID       CHARACTER VARYING(15) NOT NULL,
        RESID           CHARACTER VARYING(15) NOT NULL,
        RELATIONSHIP    CHARACTER VARYING(20));

CREATE TABLE DESCRIBES
        (ITEMCODE       CHARACTER VARYING(100) NOT NULL,
        QNAME           CHARACTER VARYING(100) NOT NULL,
        RELPOS          INTEGER,
        INHERITED       CHARACTER VARYING(20));

-- ** A PR between QUERY and VIEW entities **
CREATE TABLE MAPPEDTO
        (QNAME          CHARACTER VARYING(100) NOT NULL,
        VNAME           CHARACTER VARYING(100) NOT NULL,
        ADDEDBY         CHARACTER VARYING(10),
        DATEADDED       CHARACTER VARYING(10),
        MODIFBY         CHARACTER VARYING(10),
```

```
        LASTMOD          CHARACTER VARYING(10),
        NUMMODS          INTEGER);

-- ** A PR between ITEM and VIEW entities **
CREATE TABLE BELONGTO
        (ITEMCODE        CHARACTER VARYING(100) NOT NULL,
        VNAME            CHARACTER VARYING(100) NOT NULL,
        RELPOS           INTEGER,
        INPKEY           INTEGER,
        POSINPK          INTEGER);

-- *
CREATE TABLE RELATES
        (CNAME           CHARACTER VARYING(20) NOT NULL,
        QNAME            CHARACTER VARYING(20) NOT NULL,
        DIRECTION        INTEGER);

-- *
CREATE TABLE CONTAINS
        (CNAME           CHARACTER VARYING(20) NOT NULL,
        RNAME            CHARACTER VARYING(20) NOT NULL,
        RELORDER         INTEGER);

-- ** A PR between QUERY and RULE entities **
CREATE TABLE APPLIES
        (QNAME           CHARACTER VARYING(20) NOT NULL,
        RNAME            CHARACTER VARYING(20) NOT NULL,
        RELORDER         INTEGER,
        INHERITED        CHARACTER VARYING(20));

-- ** A PR between ACTION and RULE entities **
CREATE TABLE ACTOF
        (RNAME           CHARACTER VARYING(20) NOT NULL,
        ACTID            CHARACTER VARYING(10) NOT NULL,
        RELORDER         INTEGER);

-- ** A PR between FACT and SOFTWARE RESOURCES entities **
CREATE TABLE COMPUTES
        (FACTID          CHARACTER VARYING(10) NOT NULL,
        FUNCTID          CHARACTER VARYING(16) NOT NULL,
        PARID            CHARACTER VARYING(10),
        PARORDER         INTEGER);

-- ** A PR between ACTION and SOFTWARE entities **
CREATE TABLE CALLS
        (ACTID           CHARACTER VARYING(10) NOT NULL,
        PROCID           CHARACTER VARYING(10) NOT NULL,
        PARID            CHARACTER VARYING(10),
        PARORDER         INTEGER);
```

```
-- ** A recursive PR on ITEM entity **
CREATE TABLE EQUIVALENT
        (ITEMCODE      CHARACTER VARYING(10) NOT NULL,
        EQITEMCODE     CHARACTER VARYING(10) NOT NULL,
        CONVERT_BY     CHARACTER VARYING(20),
        REVERSE_BY     CHARACTER VARYING(20),
        ADDEDBY        CHARACTER VARYING(10),
        DATEADDED      CHARACTER VARYING(10),
        MODIFBY        CHARACTER VARYING(10),
        LASTMOD        CHARACTER VARYING(10),
        NUMMODS        INTEGER);

-- ** A PR between ITEM and SOFTWARE entities **
CREATE TABLE STOREDIN
        (ITEMCODE      CHARACTER VARYING(10) NOT NULL,
        RESID          CHARACTER VARYING(15) NOT NULL,
        RELPOS         INTEGER);

-- ** A PR between SOFTWARE and HARDWARE entities **
CREATE TABLE RESIDESAT
        (RESID         CHARACTER VARYING(15) NOT NULL,
        SERIALNO       CHARACTER VARYING(10) NOT NULL,
        PATH           CHARACTER VARYING(45),
        INVOKECOM      CHARACTER VARYING(45));

CREATE SEQUENCE factid;
CREATE SEQUENCE condid;
CREATE SEQUENCE rname;
```

2.2 Description of GIRD and Blackboard Structural Elements

This list is derived from the original Metadatabase research (Bouziane 1991; Cheung 1991); however the meta-entities and meta-relationships are shared with the Blackboard and so are repeated here for convenience. The new and modified attributes that are contributed by the Blackboard structure have their attributes emboldened.

Table B-1: Description of GIRD and Blackboard Structural Elements

RELATION	(Primary Key, Attribute₁, ..., Attributeₙ)
Action	(Actid, acttype, factid, addedby, dateadded, modifby, lastmod, nummods)
Actof	(Actid, Rname, relorder, addedby, dateadded, modifby, lastmod, nummods)
Application	(Applname, descript, addedby, dateadded, modifby, lastmod, nummods, userid)

Applies	(<u>Sname</u>, <u>Rname</u>, relorder)
Appluser	(<u>Applname</u>, <u>Userid</u>, password, accesscode, addedby, dateadded, modifby, lastmod, nummods)
Belongto	(<u>Itemcode</u>,<u>Vname</u>, relpos, inpkey, posinpk)
Calls	(<u>Actid</u>, <u>Procid</u>, Parid, parorder)
Computes	(<u>Factid</u>, <u>Functid</u>,Parid, parorder)
Condition	(<u>Condid</u>, leftfact, operator, rightfact, addedby, dateadded, modifby, lastmod, nummods)
Contains	(<u>Cname</u>, <u>Rname</u>, relorder, addedby, dateadded, modifby, lastmod, nummods)
Context	(<u>Cname</u>, applname, descript, xcoord, ycoord, addedby, dateadded, modifby, lastmod, nummods)
Describes	(<u>Itemcode</u>, <u>Qname</u>, relpos)
Ent-Rel	(<u>ERname</u>, ertype, descript, akey, addedby, dateadded, modifby, lastmod, nummods)
Equivalent	(<u>Itemcode</u>, <u>EqItemcode</u>, rname, addedby, dateadded)
Fact	(<u>Factid</u>, factname, facttype, factvalue)
Hardware Resource	(<u>Serialno</u>, hname, htype, descript, location, nodename, nodeaddr, manufacturer, purchby, datepurch, addedby, dateadded, modifby, lastmod, nummods, userid)
Integrity	(<u>Intname</u>, inttype, descript, master, slave, addedby, dateadded, modifby, lastmod, nummods)
Item	(<u>Itemcode</u>, itemname, itemtype, descript, format, length, domain, defvalue, addedby, dateadded, modifby, lastmod, nummods, applname)
Mappedto	(<u>Qname</u>, <u>Vname</u>, addedby, dateadded, modifby, lastmod, nummods)
Moduleof	(<u>Resid</u>, <u>Subresid</u>, relationship)
Namedas	(<u>Vname</u>, <u>Sysname</u>, localname)
Query	(<u>Qname</u>, Sysname. Qtype, timestamp)
Relates	(<u>Cname</u>, <u>Qname</u>, direction)
Residesat	(<u>Resid</u>, <u>Serialno</u>, path, invokecom, addedby, dateadded, modifby, lastmod, nummods)
Rule	(<u>Rname</u>, rtype, descript, condid, addedby, dateadded, modifby, lastmod, nummods)
Software Resource	(<u>Resid</u>, resname, extension, restype, descript, sizevalue, sizeunit, coding, developedby, addedby, dateadded, modifby, lastmod, nummods)
Storedin	(<u>Itemcode</u>, <u>Resid</u>, relpos)
Subject	(<u>Sname</u>, descript, xcoord, ycoord, addedby, dateadded, modifby, lastmod, nummods, supersname, applname, fileid)
System	(<u>Sysname</u>, host, timestamp)
User	(<u>Userid</u>, username, class, position, phone, office, address, addedby, dateadded, modifby, lastmod, nummods)
Uses	(<u>Applname</u>, <u>Resid</u>, dataorg, addedby, dateadded, modifby, lastmod,

	nummods)
View	(<u>V</u>name, Vtype, descript)

2.3 Definitions of Metadatabase and Blackboard Meta-Attributes

This list is derived from the original Metadatabase research (Bouziane 1991; Cheung 1991); however the attributes are shared with the Blackboard and so are repeated here for convenience. The new attributes that are contributed by the Blackboard structure have their description emboldened.

Table B-2: Definitions of Metadatabase and Blackboard Meta-Attributes

META-ATTRIBUTE	DESCRIPTION
accesscode	An attribute of the meta-PR appluser that identifies a user's authorized data access level; e.g., Read (R), Write (W), Execute (E), Delete (D).
actid	Unique identifier (primary key) for meta-entity ACTION.
acttype	Class of consequences of the production rule. Ex. Takes on a value of 0 if result of rule is binding of a fact or a value of 1 for a procedure call.
addedby	Name/initials of a modeler or information administrator who entered the meta-entity or relationship into the GIRD. Provides an audit trail.
address	Home address of a user. Attribute of meta-entity USER.
akey	Alternative primary-key(s) for an ENT-REL base relation.
applname	Unique name (primary key) for an application.
class	Classification scheme for end-users; can serve to control privileges and data access.
cname	Unique name (primary key) for the meta-entity CONTEXT.
coding	The type of physical representation of a software resource; e.g., Pascal or LISP for program code; or ASCII, VSAM, or ISAM for data files.
condid	Unique identifier (primary key) for meta-entity CONDITION. Also an attribute of meta-entity RULE.
dataorg	Indicates how the data is organized in an application in meta-PR USES.
dateadded	Date that instance of meta-entity or meta-relationship was added to GIRD.
datepurch	Date on which a hardware resource was purchased/acquired.
defvalue	Default value, if any, for a meta-entity ITEM.
descript	Description of all defined meta-entities and meta-relationships.
developedby	The name of the firm or person who developed a software resource.
direction	Indicates how the link (data flows) between a CONTEXT and SUBJECT

	is directed graphically. (i.e.; 1 = toward SUBJECT; 2 = toward CONTEXT; 3 =bidirectional; nil = none)
domain	The set of values that can be assigned to a data item (meta-entity ITEM).
eqitemcode	Synonym for itemcode in meta-PR Equivalent.
ername	Unique name (primary key) for meta-entity ENT-REL.
ertype	The type of ENT-REL; takes on a value of "OE" or "PR" corresponding to an operational entity and plural relationship respectively.
extension	The file-name extension (if any) for a software resource.
factid	Unique system-generated identifier (primary key) for meta-entity FACT. Also, an attribute of meta-entity ACTION.
factname	Attribute of a fact that is either an itemcode or an expression (condid).
facttype	Attribute of a fact that indicates how the value of the fact is to be assigned: 0 if the fact value is to be retrieved from a local database, 1 if it is the result of an expression evaluation, and 2 if it is computed by a function call.
factvalue	The calculated or referenced value, or a constant, that binds a fact during the rule inference process.
fileid	Attribute of meta-entity SUBJECT. Synonym for resid.
format	The data item representation type. Attribute of meta-entity ITEM. Examples: Character (C), Integer (I), Real (R), BCD (B), EPCDIC (E), etc.
functid	Synonym of resid; identifies the function to be called for binding a fact. Key field in meta-PR Computes.
hname	Model number or name of a hardware resource.
htype	The type of hardware. Attribute of meta-entity HARDWARE RESOURCE. Examples: line-printer, mainframe, mini-, micro-computer, harddisk, etc.
inpkey	A flag (boolean value) indicating whether or not a data item is part of the primary key of ENT-REL. Attribute of meta-PR belongto.
intname	Unique name (primary key) for an integrity constraint.
inttype	The type of integrity constraint, either "FR" or "MR" corresponding to functional relationship or mandatory relationship respectively.
invokecom	The command to invoke a software resource on a hardware resource. Attribute of meta-PR residesat.
itemcode	Unique system-generated identifier (primary key) for a data element (metaentity ITEM).
itemname	The name of a data item in meta-entity ITEM.
itemtype	An attribute of meta-entity ITEM to indicate whether the data item is "persistent" (exists in at least in one local DB) or is generated at runtime.
lastmod	Date of last modification of GIRD meta-entities and meta-relationships.
leftfact	Synonym of factid and represents the left operand of an expression.
length	The length of a data item. May refer to length in character positions or bytes depending upon implementation.

localname	Attribute of meta-PR namedas.
location	Physical location for meta-entity HARDWARE RESOURCE.
manufacturer	The manufacturer of a hardware resource.
master	An attribute of meta-entity INTEGRITY which, in the case of an FRtype, plays the role of determinant; and in the case of an MRtype, plays the role of owner.
modifby	Identifier (name or initials) of an individual who last modified an instance of a given meta-relation.
nodeaddress	Network address for a hardware resource.
nodename	Network "node" name for a hardware resource.
nummods	Number of modifications to a meta-entity. This attribute is in all meta-entities and most meta-PRs.
office	Office location or address of meta-entity USER.
operator	The logical operator in antecedent of a production rule. This includes the set of arithmetic and set operators.
parid	Synonym of factid which represents a parameter of a function in meta-PR Calls.
parorder	The relative position of the parameter in a function/procedure parameter list.
path	Path to top level directory in which a software resource resides on a hardware resource.
password	The password to an application in meta-PR appluser.
phone	Business telephone number of a user.
posinpkey	The relative position of a data item field in the primary key of ENT-REL.
position	Organizational position of the user; e.g., president, DBA, data-entry clerk.
procid	Synonym of resid, it identifies the procedure to be called for a rule action.
purchby	Identifier of individual responsible for the purchase of the hardware resource.
qname	Unique identifier (primary key) for the meta-entity QUERY
qtype	The type of query, i.e. REQUEST or OFFER
relationship	The relationship among software resources; in meta-PR moduleof.
relorder	Relative order (sequence) of a rule within a SUBJECT or CONTEXT — or of a condition in a rule.
relpos	Relative position of a data item in meta-entity ENT-REL.
resid	A unique identifier (primary key) for meta-entity SOFTWARE RESOURCE
resname	Title/name of a software resource.
restype	Software resource type; e.g., program, data file, network, document.

rightfact	Synonym of factid and represents the right side operand of an expression.
rname	Unique name (primary key) for meta-entity RULE.
rtype	The type of rule; e.g., Modeling (M), Operating (O), Production (P), etc.
serialno	The unique identifier (primary key) for meta-entity HARDWARE RESOURCE.
sizeunit	The unit of measure for describing storage of a software resource; e.g., KBytes, blocks, cylinders, pages, etc.
sizevalue	Quantity of units of storage for a specified software resource (expressed in size units).
slave	An attribute of meta-entity INTEGRITY which, in the case of an FRtype, plays the role of determined; and in the case of an MRtype, plays the role of owned.
sname	Unique name (primary key) of meta-entity SUBJECT.
subresid	A synonym for resid. Key field in meta-PR moduleof.
ssname	The upper-level (if any) subject name for meta-entity SUBJECT.
sysname	Unique identifier (primary key) for the meta-entity SYSTEM
timestamp	Current date and time a tuple is added to the relation.
userid	Unique identifier (primary key) for meta-entity USER.
username	Full name of a user in meta-entity USER.
vname	Unique identifier (primary key) for the meta-entity VIEW
xcoord	X-coordinate of the graphical representation of a SUBJECT or CONTEXT.
y coord	Y-coordinate of the graphical representation of a SUBJECT or CONTEXT.

References

Ahmed, R., J. Albert, et al. (1993). An overview of Pegasus. RIDE-IMS '93, Thirrd International Workshop on Research Issues in Data Engineering: Interoperability in Multidatabase Systems. April 19-20, 1993. Vienna, Austria. IEEE-CS.

Ahmed, R., P. DeSmedt, et al. (1991). "The Pegasus heterogeneous multidatabase system." Computer 24(12): 19-27.

Babin, G. (1993). Adaptiveness in Information Systems Integration. Unpublished Ph.D. Thesis. Decision Sciences & Engineering Systems Dept. Troy. Rensselaer Polytechnic Institute.

Babin, G. (2004). CompTools : A Compiler Generator for C and Java. Montreal, Quebec: HEC Montréal. Cahier de recherche no. 04-09.

Babin, G. and C. Hsu (1996). "Decomposition of knowledge for concurrent processing." IEEE Transactions on Knowledge and Data Engineering 8(5): 758-772.

Baker, A. (1998). "A Survey of Factory Control Algorithms That Can Be Implemented in a Multi-Agent Hierarchy: Dispatching, Scheduling, and Pull." Journal of Manufacturing Systems 17(4): 297-320.

Batini, C., M. Lenzerini, et al. (1986). "A comparative analysis of methodologies for database schema integration." ACM Computing Surveys 18(4): 323-364.

Bayardo, R. J., Jr., W. Bohrer, et al. (1997). InfoSleuth: agent-based semantic integration of information in open and dynamic environments. Proceedings ACM SIGMOD International Conference on Management of Data. May 13-15, 1997. Tucson, Arizona, USA. ACM.

Beynon-Davies, P., L. Bonde, et al. (1997). "A Collaborative Schema Integration System." Computer Supported Cooperative Work: The Journal of Collaborative Computing 6(1): 1-18.

Bouziane, M. (1991). Metadata Modeling and Management. Unpublished Ph.D. Thesis. Computer Science Dept. Troy. Rensselaer Polytechnic Institute.

Braumandl, R., M. Keidl, et al. (2001). "ObjectGlobe: Ubiquitous query processing on the Internet." The VLDB Journal 10(1): 48-71.

Bushnell, J. (2004). "California's electricity crisis: a market apart?" Energy Policy 32(9): 1045-1052.

Buyya, R., D. Abramson, et al. (2002). "Economic models for resource management and scheduling in Grid computing." Concurrency and Computation: Practice and Experience 14(13-15): 1507-1542.

Carey, M. J., L. M. Haas, et al. (1995). Towards heterogeneous multimedia information systems: the Garlic approach. Proceedings RIDE-DOM '95: Fifth International Workshop on Research Issues in Data Engineering-Distributed Object Management. March 6-7, 1995. Taipei, Taiwan. IEEE-CS.

Cesta, A., A. Oddi, et al. (2000). Iterative Flattening: A Scalable Method for Solving Multi-Capacity Scheduling Problems. Proceedings of the Seventeenth National Conference on Artificial Intelligence and Twelfth Conference on on Innovative Applications of Artificial Intelligence. July 30 - August 3, 2000. Austin, Texas, USA. AAAI Press / The MIT Press.

Chamberlin, D. (2002). "XQuery: An XML query language." IBM Systems Journal 41(4): 597-615.

Cheung, W. (1991). The model-assisted global query system. Unpublished Dissertation. Unpublished Ph.D. Thesis. Decision Sciences & Engineering Systems Dept. Troy. Rensselaer Polytechnic Institute.

Cheung, W. and C. Hsu (1996). "The model-assisted global query system for multiple databases in distributed enterprises." ACM Transactions on Information Systems (TOIS) 14(4): 421-470.

Cingil, I. and A. Dogac (2001). "An Architecture for Supply Chain Integration and Automation on the Internet." Distributed and Parallel Databases 10(1): 59-102.

Clarke, I., S. G. Miller, et al. (2002). "Protecting Free Expression Online with Freenet." IEEE Internet Computing 6(1): 40-49.

Clearwater, S. H. (1996). Market-based control : a paradigm for distributed resource allocation / editor, Scott H. Clearwater. Singapore; River Edge, NJ, World Scientific.

Collet, C., M. N. Huhns, et al. (1991). "Resource integration using a large knowledge base in Carnot." Computer 24(12): 55-62.

Collins, J., C. Bilot, et al. (2001). "Decision processes in agent-based automated contracting." IEEE Internet Computing 5(2): 61-72.

Collins, J., B. Youngdahl, et al. (1998). A market architecture for multi-agent contracting. Second International Conference on Autonomous Agents (Agents '98). May 9-13, 1998. Minneapolis/St. Paul. ACM Press.

CommerceOne (2003). http://www.commerceone.com.

Conway, R., W. Maxwell, et al. (1967). Theory of Scheduling. Reading, MA, Addison-Wesley.

Coppersmith, D. and P. Raghavan (1989). "Multidimensional On-line Bin Packing: Algorithms and Worst-Case Analysis." Operations Research Letters 8(1): 17-20.

Covisint (2004). http://www.covisint.com.

Dayal, U., M. Hsu, et al. (2001). Business Process Coordination: State of the Art, Trends, and Open Issues. VLDB 2001, Proceedings of 27th International Conference on Very Large Data Bases. September 11-14, 2001. Roma, Italy. Morgan Kaufmann.

Di Noia, T., E. Di Sciascio, et al. (2000). A system for principled matchmaking in an electronic marketplace. Twelfth International World Wide Web Conference. 20-24 May 2003. Budapest, Hungary.

Elmasri, R. and S. Navathe (2000). Fundamentals of database systems. 3rd. Reading, Mass., Addison-Wesley.

Finin, T., R. Fritzson, et al. (1994). KQML as an Agent Communication Language. Proceedings of the Third International Conference on Information and Knowledge Management. December 1994. Gaithersburg, Maryland. ACM Press.

Florescu, D. and D. Kossmann (1999). "Storing and Querying XML Data using an RDBMS." IEEE Data Engineering Bulletin 22(3): 27-34.

Fremantle, P., S. Weerawarana, et al. (2002). "Enterprise Services." Communications of the ACM 45(10): 77-82.

Garcia-Molina, H., J. D. Ullman, et al. (2002). Database systems : the complete book. Upper Saddle River, NJ, Prentice Hall.

Haas, L. M., E. T. Lin, et al. (2002). "Data integration through database federation." IBM Systems Journal 41(4): 578-596.

Haas, L. M., R. J. Miller, et al. (1999). "Transforming Heterogeneous Data with Database Middleware: Beyond Integration." IEEE Data Engineering Bulletin 22(1): 31-36.

Hendler, J. (2001). "Agents and the Semantic Web." Intelligent Systems, IEEE [see also IEEE Expert] 16(2): 30-37.

Heragu, S. S., R. J. Graves, et al. (2002). "Intelligent agent based framework for manufacturing systems control." Systems, Man and Cybernetics, Part A, IEEE Transactions on 32(1083-4427): 560-573.

Hochbaum, D. S. and D. B. Shmoys (1987). "Using Dual Approixmation Algorithms for Scheduling Problems: Theoretical and Practical Results." Journal of the ACM, 34(1): 144-162.

Hsu, C. (1996). Enterprise integration and modeling : the metadatabase approach / by Cheng Hsu. Boston, Kluwer Academic Publishers.

Hsu, C. (2002). A Market Mechanism for Information Enterprise Resource Allocation. Troy: Decision Sciences and Engineering Systems, Rensselaer Polytechnic Institute. TR 38-02-493. 18 p.

Hsu, C. and G. Babin (1993). A Rule-Oriented Concurrent Architecture to Effect Adaptiveness for Integrated Manufacturing Enterprises. International Conference on Industrial Engineering and Production Management. June 1993. Mons, Belgium.

Hsu, C., G. Babin, et al. (1992). "Metadatabase Modeling for Enterprise Information Integration." Journal of Systems Integration 2(1): 5-39.

Hsu, C., M. Bouziane, et al. (1991). "Information Resources Management in Heterogeneous, Distributed Environments: A Metadatabase Approach." IEEE Transactions on Software Engineering 17(6): 604-624.

Hsu, C. and C. Carothers (2003). A Self-Scheduling Model Using Agent-Base, Peer-to-Peer Negotiation, and Open Common Schema. 17th International Conference on Production Research. 3rd August-7th August 2003. Blacksburg, VA.

Hsu, C. and C. Carothers (2004). A Design for Enterprises Collaboration: Information Sensing, Exchange, and Fusion. Troy: Decision Sciences and Engineering Systems, Rensselaer Polytechnic Institute. TR: 38-04-508.

Hsu, C., C. Carothers, et al. (2005). "A Market Mechanism for Participatory Global Query: A First Step of Enterprise Resource Allocation." Information Technology and Management(forthcoming in 2005).

Hsu, C. and S. Pant (2000). Planning for Electronic Commerce and Enterprises: A Reference Model. Boston, Kluwer Academic Publishers.

Hsu, C., Y. Tao, et al. (1993). "Paradigm Translations in Integrating Manufacturing Information Using a Meta-Model." Ingénierie des systèmes d'information 1(3): 325-352.

Keidl, M., A. Kreutz, et al. (2002). A Publish & Subscribe Architecture for Distributed Metadata Management. Proceedings of the 18th International Conference on Data Engineering. 26 February - 1 March 2002. San Jose, CA. IEEE Computer Society.

Kossmann, D. (2000). "The state of the art in distributed query processing." ACM Computing Surveys 32(4): 422-469.

Kurbel, K. and L. Loutchko (2003). "Towards multi-agent electronic marketplaces: what is there and what is missing?" The Knowledge Engineering Review 18(1): 33-46.

Kuttner, R. (2002). "Free Markets are Great-But Not for Electricity." Business Week(3803): 34.

Kwiat, K. (2002). "Using Markets to Engineer Resource Management for the Information Grid." Information Systems Frontiers 4(1): 55-62.

Lenat, D. B. (1995). "CYC: a large-scale investment in knowledge infrastructure." Communications of the ACM 38(11): 33-38.

Litwin, W. (1985). An overview of the multidatabase system MRDSM. Proceedings of the 13th ACM Annual Conference, The range of computing : mid-80's perspective. October 14-16, 1985. Denver, Colorado. ACM.

Liu, J. and M. Vincent (2003). Query translation from XSLT to SQL. Seventh International Database Engineering and Applications Symposium (IDEAS'03). July 16 - 18, 2003. Hong Kong, SAR. IEEE-CS.

Maes, P., R. H. Guttman, et al. (1999). "Agents that buy and sell." Communications of the ACM 42(3): 81-ff.

McIlraith, S. A., T. C. Son, et al. (2001). "Semantic Web services." Intelligent Systems, IEEE [see also IEEE Expert] 16(2): 46-53.

Mena, E., A. Illarramendi, et al. (2000). "OBSERVER: An Approach for Query Processing in Global Information Systems Based on Interoperation Across Pre-Existing Ontologies." Distributed and Parallel Databases 8(2): 223-271.

Nandula, M. and S. P. Dutta (2000). "Performance Evaluation of an Auction-Based Manufacturing System Using Colored Petri Nets." International Journal of Production Research 38(38): 2155-2171.

Özsu, M. T. and P. Valduriez (1991). Principles of distributed database systems. Englewood Cliffs, N.J., Prentice Hall.

Parameswaran, M., A. Susarla, et al. (2001). "P2P networking: an information sharing alternative." IEEE Computer 34(7): 31-38.

Parunak, H. (2001). Agents in Overalls: Experiences and Issues in the Development and Deployment of Industrial Agent-Based Systems. Ann Arbor, MI 48113-4001: ERIM CEC Report, P.O. Box 134001.

Prabhu, V. (2000). "Performance of Real-Time Distributed Arrival Time Control in Heterogeneous Manufacturing Systems." IIE Transactions 32(4): 323-331.

Rahm, E. and P. A. Bernstein (2001). "A survey of approaches to automatic schema matching." The VLDB Journal 10(4): 334-350.

Rahwan, I., R. Kowalczyk, et al. (2002). Intelligent agents for automated one-to-many e-commerce negotiation. Proceedings of the twenty-fifth Australasian conference on Computer science. January 2002. Melbourne, Victoria, Australia. Australian Computer Society, Inc.

Ribeiro, C. C., C. D. Ribeiro, et al. (1997). "Query Optimization in Distributed Relation Databases." Journal of Heuristics 3(1): 5-23.

Rodríguez-Martínez, M. and N. Roussopoulos (2000). MOCHA: a self-extensible database middleware system for distributed data sources. Proceedings of the 2000 ACM SIGMOD International Conference on Management of Data. May 16-18, 2000. Dallas, Texas. ACM.

Sairamesh, J., R. Mohan, et al. (2002). "A platform for business-to-business sell-side, private exchanges and marketplaces." IBM Systems Journal 41(2): 242-252.

Sheth, A. and J. A. Larson (1990). "Federated Database Systems for Managing Distributed Heterogeneous and Autonomous Systems." ACM Computing Surveys 22(3): 183-236.

Silberschatz, A., H. F. Korth, et al. (2002). Database system concepts. 4th. Boston, McGraw-Hill.

Sim, K. M. and R. Chan (2000). "A brokering protocol for agent-based e-commerce." Systems, Man and Cybernetics, Part C, IEEE Transactions on 30(4): 474-484.

Sim, K. M. and E. Wong (2001). "Toward market-driven agents for electronic auction." Systems, Man and Cybernetics, Part A, IEEE Transactions on 31(6): 474-484.

Singh, M. P., P. E. Cannata, et al. (1997). "The Carnot Heterogeneous Database Project: Implemented Applications." Distributed and Parallel Databases 5(2): 207-225.

Stonebraker, M., P. M. Aoki, et al. (1996). "Mariposa: A Wide Area Distributed Database System." The VLDB Journal 5(1): 48-63.

Sundaram, M. and S. S. Y. Shim (2001). Infrastructure for B2B exchanges with RosettaNet. 3rd IEEE International Workshop on Advanced Issues of E-Commerce and Web-Based Information Systems (WECWIS 2001). 21–22 June 2001. San Jose, CA. IEEE-CS.

Swaminathan, J., S. F. Smith, et al. (1998). "Modeling Supply Chain Dynamics: a Multi-Agent Approach." Decision Sciences 29(3): 607-632.

Sycara, K., M. Klusch, et al. (1999). "Dynamic Service Matchmaking Among Agents in Open Information Environments." Journal ACM SIGMOD Record 28(1): 47-53.

Sycara, K., J. Lu, et al. (1999). Matchmaking among Heterogeneous Agents on the Internet. Proceedings of the 1999 AAAI Spring Symposium on Intelligent Agents in Cyberspace. 22-24 March 1999. Stanford University, USA.

Sycara, K., M. Paolucci, et al. (2003). "The RETSINA MAS Infrastructure." Autonomous Agents and Multi-Agent Systems 7(1-2): 29-48.

The PostgreSQL Global Development Group (2005). "PostgreSQL 7.4.7 Documentation, http://www.postgresql.org/docs/7.4/static/index.html."

Tsalgatidou, A. and T. Pilioura (2002). "An Overview of Standards and Related Technology in Web Services." Distributed and Parallel Databases 12(2-3): 135-162.

Userland Software (2005). "XML-RPC, http://www.xmlrpc.com/."

W3C (2004). Extensible Markup Language (XML), http://www.w3.org/XML/.

W3C (2004). XML Path Language (XPath) Version 1.0, http://www.w3.org/TR/xpath.

W3C (2004). XSL Transformations (XSLT) Version 1.0, http://www.w3.org/TR/xslt.

W3C (2005). "Simple Object Access Protocol (SOAP), http://www.w3.org/TR/soap/."

Want, I. N., N. J. Fiddian, et al. (2001). Market-Based Agent Allocation in Global Information Systems. Proceedings of the fifth international conference on Autonomous Agents. May 28 - June 01, 2001. Montreal, Quebec, Canada.

Waterhouse, S., D. M. Doolin, et al. (2002). "Distributed search in P2P networks." Internet Computing, IEEE 6(1): 68-72.

Wisner, J. D. and K. C. Tan (2000). "Supply Chain Management and Its Impact on Purchasing." The Journal of Supply Chain Managment 36(4): 33-42.

Index